SCOTTISH AND IRISH DIARIES

KENNIKAT PRESS SCHOLARLY REPRINTS

Ralph Adams Brown, Senior Editor

Series In

IRISH HISTORY AND CULTURE

Under the General Editorial Supervision of
Gilbert A. Cahill
Professor of History, State University of New York

SCOTTISH AND IRISH DIARIES

FROM THE SIXTEENTH TO THE
NINETEENTH CENTURY
WITH AN INTRODUCTION
BY
ARTHUR PONSONBY, M.P.

As I walked by myself
I talked to myself
and thus myself said to me

(motto on first page of Sir Walter Scott's Journal.)

KENNIKAT PRESS
Port Washington, N. Y./London

SCOTTISH AND IRISH DIARIES

First published in 1927
Reissued in 1970 by Kennikat Press
Library of Congress Catalog Card No: 70-102626
SBN 8046-0802-4

Manufactured by Taylor Publishing Company   Dallas, Texas

KENNIKAT SERIES IN IRISH HISTORY AND CULTURE

PREFACE

IN dealing with Scottish diaries I have been greatly assisted by the admirable way in which many of them have been carefully edited and reproduced in the volumes of Scottish learned Societies. I am specially indebted to Sir James Balfour Paul (late Lyon King-of-Arms), the editor of Ridpath's diary, for his help and advice and for drawing my attention to diaries which otherwise I should have missed.

Irish diaries have been more difficult to discover. Miss Edith M. Stopford has given me valuable assistance and I have been furnished with lists by Mr. R. I. Best, Librarian of the National Library of Ireland.

My thanks are due to those who have kindly allowed me to examine manuscript diaries. The publisher's consent has been obtained in a few cases where extracts are given from recently published books.

Although about seventy diaries are referred to in this volume they must be regarded as a selection and by no means as an exhaustive collection.

A. P.

SHULBREDE PRIORY
   SUSSEX
     1927

CONTENTS

SCOTTISH AND IRISH DIARIES

INTRODUCTION

AND NOTES ON MIÑOR SCOTTISH AND IRISH DIARIES

THE division of the studies of diaries contained in Classifica- these volumes into English, Scottish and Irish has tion of English been adopted merely for convenience' sake. There Scottish, are no fundamental differences in the habit of diary writing and Irish diaries in the three parts of the United Kingdom or for a matter of that in any part of the world. Sufficient English diaries were discovered to fill a volume and indeed two and it therefore appeared best to keep the Scottish and Irish diaries for a separate volume. Even so, there are many diaries the nationality of which is questionable. Dr. Rutty lived all his life in Dublin, but he is included in the English series. Swift was not an Irishman by birth, but I have put the Journal to Stella into this volume. Elizabeth Freke was only connected with Ireland through her husband, but her diary has been printed in the collection of the Cork Archæological Society and this extraordinary and amusing journal has been put among the Irish. Other instances might be given in which objection may be taken to the classification and it is as well therefore to explain that the division has no significance whatever and has only been used as a handy method of dealing with the vast mass of material I have had at my disposal.

Nevertheless the Scot may be regarded as specially addicted
to diary writing. The religious motive instilled by the
Covenanters was responsible for producing many diaries.
There must have been an enormous number of these in existence at one time. Two good instances are given in the
diaries of Lord Wariston and Alexander Brodie. Scottish
learned societies have been at great pains to reproduce with
careful notes and prefaces many old diaries of historical
interest, and so made them easily accessible. In neither
Scotland nor Ireland have I delved quite so deep outside
the sphere of printed books as I have in England, but I have
found sufficient representative diaries to fill a volume. In
quality it will be noted the level is in no way lower than in
England both as regards the more important diaries and the
minor journals of insignificant people.

If I express a preference for Sir Walter Scott's diary over
any other out of the large number I have read, I do not
think I shall stand alone in my preference. The excellence
of that diary is seriously impaired by the unavoidable expedient of giving extracts. You must live with Sir Walter
day by day in order to get to know him and enjoy the wonderful charm of his intercourse.

Tom Moore's is a good Irish diary. He and Scott were
contemporaries. Very rarely can one catch two diarists
meeting and both giving an account of the event and of one
another. We get very near to it, indeed we actually find it,
in the case of Scott and Moore.

Moore's visit to Scott at Abbotsford was concluded about
the second week in November, 1825. Scott began his Journal
on November 20. It would be too much to say that Moore
encouraged Scott to write a diary. But they talked a great
deal about Byron and undoubtedly Byron's diary must have
been the subject of conversation.

The Ravenna diary was sent by Mr. Murray to Lockhart
a day or two later, and Scott then and there procured a
thick quarto volume bound in vellum and in his first entry
mentions approvingly Byron's method.

Moore's references to his visit are in his light style, a recital
of the particular and actual with appropriate illustration and

anecdote. On the other hand, Scott, when he begins his diary, is full of Moore and we get a most charming description of him :

> There is a manly frankness and perfect ease and good breeding about him which is delightful. Not the least touch of the poet or the pedant. A little—very little man . . . his countenance is decidedly plain but the expression is so very animated especially in speaking or singing that it is far more interesting than the finest features could have rendered it.
>
> I was aware that Byron had often spoken both in private society and in his Journal of Moore and myself in the same breath and with some sort of regard ; so I was curious to see what there could be in common betwixt us, Moore having lived so much in the gay world, I in the country and with people of business and sometimes with politicians ; Moore a scholar, I none ; he a musician and artist, I without knowledge of a note ; he a democrat, I an aristocrat— with many other points of difference ; besides his being an Irishman, I a Scotchman and both tolerably national. Yet there is a point of resemblance and a strong one. We are both good humoured fellows, who rather seek to enjoy what is going forward than to maintain our dignity as lions ; and we have both seen the world too widely and too well not to condemn in our souls the imaginary consequence of literary people who walk with their noses in the air and remind me always of the fellow whom Johnson met in an ale- house and who called himself " the great Twalmley, inventor of the floodgate iron for smoothing linen." He also enjoys the *mot pour rire* and so do I.

They certainly were kindred spirits.

Comparing the subsequent entries when they meet we find Moore recording Scott's sayings and treating him more or less as a celebrity, while Scott does little more than just men- tion Moore's presence. Moore's diary is delightful in its way, and there is room for diaries to be very delightful with- out reaching anywhere near the level of Sir Walter Scott. But Moore seldom generalizes or attempts character sketches. However, we find him reflecting after a visit with Scott to some neighbours :

> Could not help thinking during this quiet homely visit how aston- ished some of those foreigners would be, to whom the name of Sir Walter Scott is encircled with so much romance to see the quiet neighbourly manner with which he took his seat among those old maids and the familiar ease with which they treated him in return ;

no country squire with but half an idea in his head could have fallen into the gossip of a humdrum country visit more unassumingly.

The actual simultaneous entries are few and incidental, but we have sufficient of what the two men wrote freshly about one another to illustrate their mutual appreciation.

Women's diaries   Women are very well represented in this volume. We have Mrs. Carlyle's fragment, an early diary of Mary Rich and Lady Arabella Denny, the child's diary of Marjorie Flemming, and Elizabeth Freke's record which stands in a category by itself.

The lighter touches   There are plenty of light touches in the smaller diaries. I am not above being interested when I read how a seventeenth-century Lord Advocate's (Sir Thomas Hope) ruff caught fire and he ran down the passage crying for help, nor when John Fitzgerald, the Irish schoolmaster, tells us that he went to bed " very mellow." We get a sidelight on Rowland Davies's manners when we learn that his landlady objected to his " spitting about the house," and William Cunningham of Craigends with his silk stockings, broidered garters, silver buckles and numberless silver buttons shows us very clearly what a dandy he was.

Account books   Books of account are sometimes tempting although they cannot be included.   Those kept by Colin and George Campbell,[1] who were curators, are almost like diary entries.   Between 1638 and 1653 the items of expenditure are full of information.   There is a list amounting to over £2,000 of the wedding trousseau of Mistress Jean which include not only silks and satins, ribbons, silver buttons, etc., but " rich imbroithered nightcaps and slipperis," a " leaced love hod " and an " embroithered womanis sadle."

MINOR SCOTTISH DIARIES

There are a good many diaries to which separate notices have not been given which are nevertheless worth mentioning.   In some cases I have had to exclude interesting documents which are just beyond the line of definition I have drawn of a private diary.

John Lauder   For instance, I was strongly tempted to include in this

[1] *The Book of Thanes of Cawdor* (Spalding Club, 1859).

collection the so-called Journal of John Lauder, Lord Foun-
tainhall. But although it is a most excellent racy and
humorous account of travels and must have been written up
from notes taken daily, it is, in the form in which it comes
down to us, a narrative of travel and not a personal diary.
He writes about his travels in France, 1665–7, his journeys
to London, Oxford and in Scotland between 1667 and 1672.
His entertaining anecdotes and observations—some of them
very broad—give us an insight into his character, but there
is more intimate personal information to be found in the
elaborate and voluminous accounts he kept from 1670–5. A
careful analysis of these would tell us much about himself,
his wife, his household and his habits, and his taste in literature is fully illustrated by a long catalogue drawn up apparently in 1679 " of my books I bought since 1667." Considered as a travel narrative, John Lauder's is incomparably
better than those of more recent date. If only he had slipped
into the diary method and written when he was at home as
well as when he was abroad, we might have had a Scottish
Pepys.

An interesting old time-worn book [1] was kindly sent to Isabella Forbes
me which was kept by Isabella Forbes, who married William
More, an Aberdeen advocate and a member of the Scots
Parliament. In it she records the death of her father and
then the birth of her children, beginning with William in
1667. She had no less than fifteen children. One daughter
married and had children, and one son reached the age of
nineteen, the other thirteen, all died at a very early age
and she therefore turns to the end of the book in order to
record their deaths. About John, who lived till he was
nineteen, she writes fully. Her daughter and grandchildren
continued similar notes in the same book in the eighteenth
century and therefore as a family record the little leather-
bound volume is valuable, but it is not a diary.

Two soldiers' diaries may be mentioned : the one that of a
seventeenth-century military adventurer, the other that of a
great nineteenth-century general.

The diary of General Patrick Gordon, a soldier of fortune General Patrick Gordon

[1] In the possession of Mrs. Sanford, of Beeslade, Midlothian.

who was a close friend of Peter the Great, was scattered after his death, some of the volumes finding their way into the archives of the Foreign Office at Moscow. After various vicissitudes a few of the volumes were transcribed for the Spalding Society in 1859. From 1651 to the end of his life in 1699 Gordon, as a free-lance, fought for the Swedes, then for the Poles and finally settled in Russia. A full detailed diary from a man with such a career as this might be of exceptional interest. But Gordon, although he had the diarist's method very fully developed, had no powers whatever of selection, narrative, or discrimination. His trivial details are dull, his descriptions are tedious. When his historical figures appear we are disappointed (as so often happens in diaries) by hearing nothing beyond the bare mention of their names. We are told of meetings in London in 1666 with Prince Rupert, with Clarendon and with Lauderdale ; but nearly all we hear of them is that the first was very sick, that the second was confined by the gout to Berkshire House and that the third gave Sunday dinners at Highgate. Again, when he meets Queen Christian of Sweden, we are informed the conversation lasted thirty minutes, but we have not a syllable of what was said. Of his frequent meetings with Peter the Great we are told next to nothing, and in 1686 there is only a dull fragment of one of his conversations with James II, the entries being largely taken up with the cost of his meals and his washing. It is very tantalizing because he seems to have had the unique opportunities of a disinterested outsider. In setting out to keep his diary he makes one of the best expositions of motive and intention that I have come across :

I am not ignorant that it is thought as hard a task for any man to writt the story of his own lyfe and narrative of his actions as for ane artist truly to draw his owne picture yet haveing proposed to myself to writt only by way of a journall, without makeing any reflections by blameing or commending any of the passages of my lyfe (following herein the counsell of Cato. *Nec te laudaveris nec te culpaveris ipse*) I think it not uneasy ; especially not intending it for publick view, as also leaving to others, if any shall take paines to read it, the free censure of anything here done. . . . To conclude,

I cannot tell you a better or truer reason for writing this, as that
it is to please my owne fancy, not being curious of pleasing any
bodyes else, seing *omnibus placare* has been reckoned as yet among
the *impossibilia*.

The retrospective portions which precede the actual diary
are very readable, as they have a certain style, although even
in these there is no deep perception, merely superficial observation.

Sir John Moore, a Scotsman by birth, kept up practically <sub-marginal>Sir John Moore</sub-marginal>
from day to day a record of his military exploits, extending
from December 5, 1793, to December 24, 1808, three weeks
before he died, covering the British occupation of Corsica,
the capture of St. Lucia in the West Indies, the Irish Rebellion of 1798, two campaigns in Holland, the Cadiz expedition,
the conquest of Egypt, the occupation of Sicily, and the
Peninsular War. It is perhaps the most famous of all military
diaries. While he expresses himself freely and without
restraint, he confines his observations strictly to military
matters and writes for his own remembrance without a
thought of publication. For the military historian his diary
is invaluable, and in spite of its purely narrative manner,
exhibits Moore as Napier has described him, as the " stern
enemy to vice," " the steadfast friend to merit," and the
" just and faithful servant of his country." The entry which
contains his interview with Sir Gilbert Elliot, the Viceroy of
Corsica, on which occasion he was dismissed from his command, shows his remarkable power of epitomizing an involved
controversial conversation.

Among traveller diarists there is the Rev. William Mac- William
Ritchie, of Clunie, in Perthshire,[1] who made a journey through Ritchie
England in 1795. He scribbled down in shorthand descrip-
tions of what he saw, using throughout the historic present.
It is easy to read because it is quite artless and natural, but
it is not in any way remarkable.

Another travel diary is that of Dr. John Gibson, of Glas- John
Gibson

---

[1] The original manuscript is in the possession of the diarist's grand-
son, Mr. Frank B. Hopkin, of Whithorn, by whose kind permission
the diary has been examined.

gow,[1] who travelled in France and Italy in 1823–4. He has
great power of observation and expresses himself very well,
so that his detailed descriptions, made before the day of
popular guide-books, give a good picture of the sights he sees.
While there are no personal details, he allows his opinions
to penetrate from time to time. After witnessing the ceremony of the blessing of the candles at Pisa, he writes :

> I came away more and more convinced that the whole ceremony
> had more the appearance and partook more of the nature of an
> Opera Buffa (Anglice Broad farce) than a worshipping of the Deity.

And he lets himself go for a couple of pages on " the darkness
of ignorance and superstition " and the " wily priesthood."
   He shows himself to have considerable artistic perception
in the notes he makes on pictures, monuments and the beauties
of nature, although his scientific mind dwells often on mere
statistical detail.
   He is near having an adventure at Terni, where he strays
from his companions and finds himself in danger of being
surrounded—perhaps robbed or kidnapped—by suspicious-
looking goatherds and villagers. Over a dozen pages are
taken up with a very lively account of his manœuvres which
save him from danger :

> this fellow after *shouting* salutation, hinted something about the
> lateness of the evening and the loneliness of my situation, which at
> first not a little disconcerted me, but I took care that he did not
> observe it and as I saw that there was no addition making to the
> company, I thought within myself that two could play at *Cuff* if it
> should come to that.

On his way to Bologna he makes some amusing notes on
his travelling companions—an Italian in the French service,
" who to an uncultivated mind joined a pair of stentorian
lungs which he not infrequently put in use to my no small
mortification " ; his son " an uncouth uncultivated cub
about 14 who was extremely teazing from his forwardness "
and a Florentine shopkeeper with a grievance. The officer
and the shopkeeper fall out, but their quarrel

---

[1] *The Diary of a Tour through Great Britain in* 1795, by the Rev.
W. MacRitchie, 1897.

was after a season as usual brought to an amicable adjustment, not however by my interference, as I anticipated great pleasure in it coming to blows, but by their own effeminate, dull, incomprehensible, *ninny* dispositions.

The diary, which covers over 300 pages, is not intended to be anything more than a description of travels, and after the last entry on his arrival home in Glasgow he writes " Finis." Dr. Gibson would have made a good diarist if only he had realized that his daily pursuits at home would make far more interesting reading than his travels abroad. At the end of the book he keeps very elaborate weather charts as well as accounts.

I have adhered again to the decision of not including the journals of explorers which are for the most part exclusively concerned with minute observations of a scientific nature. The famous record of Dr. Livingstone (a native of Glasgow) presented great difficulty to its transcribers because when the metallic notebook which he used gave out, he wrote his notes across the type of old newspapers with a substitute for ink made out of the juice of a tree. It can be imagined how laborious was the task of deciphering these portions of the journal. Livingstone made a short entry on April 27, 1873, and died on May 1.

There is an interesting early record of public events in the sixteenth century: " The Diariey of Robert Birrell Burgess of Edinburgh containing Diverse passages of State and uthers memorable accidents," kept between 1532 to 1605. In it the movements of royalty, noteworthy incidents, hangings, burnings, etc., are briefly noted. A sample entry may be given concerning the murder of Darnley, to whom Birrell always refers as " King Henry " :

1566
On the nynth day of February being the Sunday before fastings even The King was murdered in his Lodgeing in the Kirk of Field about midnight or thereby, the said Lodgeing pertaining to Sir James Balfour provost of the said Kirk, the house was raised up from the Ground and the Kings Chamber man, named John Talzeour was found with him Lyand in the Zaird Dead, under an tree, and the King if he had not beine Cruelly wyerriet, after he sett out of the air in the Garden with his awen garters he had lived.

Sir John
Clerk

A few Scottish seventeenth-century diaries must be noted. Sir John Clerk of Penicuick (1676–1755) worked up the diary which he " was always in use to keep " into an autobiography which is printed by the Scottish History Society.

John
Lamont

The diary of John Lamont [1] (of Newton) is a chronicle of events in Scotland, particularly in Fife, from 1649 to 1671, and contains valuable genealogical notices and business entries connected with the Lamont family. There are several entries in each month, but there is no personal note whatever.

A curious single line dated record of events was found in the waste paper of the binding of an old book. The dated memoranda are supposed to have been kept by Moncrieff, Laird of Carnbee—some are in Latin. One instance may be given :

1605. Nov. 5. The trasson of gunpudder in Lundon discoverit.

The
Brodies

Alexander Brodie's diary is reviewed [2] and also his son's. A cousin of his, Alexander Brodie of Mains, also kept a diary, but only a few extracts are to be found. They consist of a recital of events and pious reflections, in one of which he exclaims, " Lord ! I have many diseases and my greatest disease is I kno' it not."

Elizabeth
Brodie

Another member of the family, Elizabeth, was also a diarist of the Covenanter type. She married James Nimmo. In settling down to keep her record she writes :

Having had many conviction for not recording more exactly the wonderful doings of the Lord about me in my pilgrimage condition, I therefore here resolve to take notice of some particulars thereof briefly as the Lord shall be pleased to help me.

We can get some idea of her strictness when she describes how she was afraid she had " sinned unto death " because one Sabbath night " when my trouble was very great there fell out a strong temptation to laughter in the family and being overcome of it I was immediately challenged though the challenge seemed to come from the Devil."

[1] *The Diary of Mr. John Lamont of Newton. Maitland Club*, 1830.
[2] See p. 45.

No entertainment can be expected from the diaries of a James family where laughter was considered " a sin unto death." Nimmo James Nimmo, her husband, was just as bad. He " perceaved with much solidness the waight of a married life." At one moment he has " some fervent inclinations to be disolved." Physical and spiritual distress react on one another :

For a considerable time thereafter my body was sore brocken by a winde in my stomock yrby my spirit was oftn discomposed.

Nimmo was born in 1654. His " narrative," which is printed by the Scottish History Society, ends in 1705, four years before his death. Elizabeth, his daughter, also wrote her journal or " narrative," which begins, " I was a blasphemer, but I obtained mercy."

Andrew Hay of Craignethan allows references to other Andrew Hay than public matters to creep into the diary which he kept punctually every day, noting not only the date but the time of day at which he wrote : " 10 May Twysday 6 acloak." Only the fifth volume [1] of what must have been a lifelong diary has survived and covers hardly a year, 1659–60. Andrew Hay was a Master of Arts, but had no profession. He was very busy, however, with Church matters, as he had allied himself with the extreme party of Covenanters. His other business was a trusteeship which he attended to with great conscientiousness. His analysis of sermons is long and exhaustive, he prays, reproaches himself and has " family and secret dutie " every evening. He makes notes whenever he himself is " unweel " and refers also to his wife's health. There are references as well to the books he reads which include " a mirrie french book." But full as the entries are, they are chiefly occupied with rather dull business and except through his style and method we do not get any close insight into his private life and character. He has a " weekly search " of self-examination and is addicted to " melancholick fitts." The most characteristic feature of the diary is the conclusion of each entry, which consists of two lines,

[1] Scottish History Society (1901).

the first summing up his moral impression of the day, the second describing the weather. A few of these may be given :

> Yet this was a good day to my soule.
> A gray cloudie day.
>
> This was but a raving day
> A gray morning and fair afternoone
>
> This was a tollerable good day
> A gurle day of blinks and showers
>
> This day was somq^t raving but had a sweet close
> A fair seasonable day
>
> Ane unfruitful day yet a blink I had
> A very foul day of raine and haill.

It is the diary of a very conscientious man, without any excessive contrition, and he is as ready to notice the " blinks " both moral and meteorological as the " gray louring " weather.

George Turnbull

The diary of another Covenanter, George Turnbull, offers little material for quotation. Turnbull, who was born in 1657, was Minister at Dalmeny, Alloa and Tyningham successively. The portion of his diary still preserved covers 1687 to 1704 and consists of entries which only concern his activities as a preacher, lecturer and hard-working pastor, with some accounts of the meetings of the General Assembly. A few weather notes and comments on public events occur, and on one occasion only, when recording the death of his son in 1703, does he indulge in any sort of introspection. In the course of this entry he writes :

> I observed that for a long time I had been very secure, formall, yea and carnall in my frame ; this security had introduced a strange withering and universall decay on all my graces in so much that Satan began to be very bold in his temptations and blasphemous suggestions.

And he begs that he may be cured of his " too trifling and unserious temper and conversation." For Monday and Saturday in the headings of his entries he writes " Moonday " and " Saturnday."

In the eighteenth century mention may be made of Sir

David Hume,[1] one of the judges of the Court of Sessions in Sir
David
Hume 1689. He kept a record of occurrences in Parliament and the Privy Council between 1701 and 1707. Although it is quite official, he has an individual style which keeps his personality to the front. A couple of entries may be given by way of illustration :

At 2 went to Parliament where there was much jangling about some expression the Duke of Athole had about his protestation which the Duke of Argyle whispered in his ear was a lye ; which being told the House by Kilmarnock took up a long time.

The next day

The Dukes of Argyle and Atholl reconciled about the difference happened yesterday marked in my diary.

He sometimes refers to his own indisposition, but on the whole it is a public record.

In the diary of the Rev. John Mill,[2] who was Minister for John
Mill many years at Dunrossness and other parishes in the Shetland Islands, may be found the record of a very strenuous life. He does not write daily, but summarizes periods, often the whole year. His energy and activity in storm and wind in covering the parishes under his ministration are kept up till he reaches a very advanced age. He writes up to his ninety-second year and continues to make notes in the Presbytery Records till within a few weeks of his death at the age of ninety-four. Born in 1712, he went to Shetland in 1743, and remained there for the rest of his life. He was a scholar and took great interest in public affairs, about which he makes many notes. He records details about his work, wrecks and storms, his family and his health, often falls into prayer and speaks of encounters with the Devil, in whose personal existence he firmly believed. We can quite well picture him as a notable character. He would mount the pulpit, we are told, with his cocked hat tied under his chin, and a bunch of flowers in his hand, and in a fine sonorous voice would address his congregation, " Ye sinners of Cunningsburgh." A good deal of the diary has been lost, some of it is retro-

[1] Bannatyne Club (1828).
[2] Scottish History Society (1889).

spective narrative, and the rest is a descriptive summary rather than a daily diary. It is carefully revised and corrected and it is not unlikely therefore that he intended it for publication.

John Campbell   There are a few sheets of a daily diary kept from September 14 to November 13, 1745, by John Campbell, a member of the Breadalbane family, who was principal cashier in the Royal Bank of Scotland. Prince Charlie's army came into Edinburgh on September 17 and remained in possession till November 1. The bank effects were transported to the Castle, and Campbell records the transactions with regard to the demands for money and his interviews with John Murray, the Prince's Secretary. The bank cashier appears to have been very accommodating. There is a note of excitement in the brief businesslike notes which concern only the crisis as it affected the bank. He mentions where he dines and often writes " dined *solus*." Although he obviously wrote only to register the particular happenings of the moment and in all probability was not a diarist otherwise, nevertheless a small personal detail creeps in which might escape the casual reader. On October 28 his account of a meeting of the court of directors ends up with the one word : " Poem." Next day " Poem continued " and after the excitement was over an entry runs :

> Din'd at home *solus*. Began to compose some lines. Paid a visit at Mr. Kinloch's. Finish'd my composure.

So the principal cashier was a poet.

George Brown   George Brown, a merchant of Glasgow, who amassed a considerable fortune, most of which was lost at the time of the American Revolution which hit Glasgow hard, kept a diary from 1745 to 1753, which was printed privately in 1856. It is rather a dull production, very Calvinistic, but there are some interesting items. He always writes " Saturnsday " for Saturday ; he is very severe on himself and reproaches himself strongly for frequently using the expression " Bless me."

Robert Paul   Robert Paul,[1] manager of the Commercial Bank of Scot-

---

[1] *Memoir of Robert Paul*, by B. Bell.

land, who helped very materially to build up the Free Church
of Scotland, kept a diary for about fifty years.   On July 8,
1866, the entries become barely legible, on July 16 he died.
He gives bald details of his occupations and there are sentences of self-correction.   He finds himself " too keen " on
politics.   " Trifles irritate me."   " I must have the last
word."   There is a period in the middle when he contents
himself with single line entries under the heading " Remark-
ables."

Henry Chancellor, who wrote daily from the age of seventeen to seventy in the nineteenth century, left his diary,
which records his doings and visits to Scottish country houses,
to the Advocates Library.   But there is neither amusement
nor edification to be derived from it.   He quite threw away
his opportunities.

Henry Chancellor

Obscure diaries are not always repaying, more especially
if only a fraction of them remains.   But any complete manuscript diary always presents points of psychological interest,
more especially if one has no other guide to the personality
of the writer.   Margaret R.,[1] who lived in Edinburgh, kept a
regular diary from 1800 to 1895.   The earlier volumes have
been lost, but from 1825 to the end it is complete except
for two years.   She wrote freely and much can be gathered of
her life and character.   We are told by one who took the
trouble to decipher the closely written pages that Margaret
" was one of those people who seem born to be unhappy
and who rather liked being unhappy.   She was a dyspeptic,
self-centred, hysterical and sensitive creature, deeply religious,
very affectionate but somewhat unstable in her friendships."
It must be remembered, however, that there are instances
of diarists confiding to and pouring out in the pages of their
private records aspects of their character and disposition
which were probably quite unsuspected by their friends.
But the despairing attitude towards life of this diarist makes
one think she must have been a little trying to associate
with.   Margaret was very methodical.   She indexed the
volumes, kept a record of her attendances at church (St.
Cuthbert's) and drew up lists of the sermons she listened to

Diary of a Medio-crity

[1] *Chambers' Journal*, April 1, 1921.   " The Diary of a Mediocrity."

and of books she read.   There are no incidents in her life,
part of which was devoted to teaching, which are of any
special interest.   She was greatly devoted to her mother,
whose death made such a lasting impression on her that for
the remainder of her life she constantly refers to it and calcu-
lates the time which had elapsed since it took place.   She
had a love affair with an elder.   He throws his arms round
her neck and kisses her warmly ;   he proposes to her, but is
rejected because he was addicted to being " merry " on
occasions and even turned up " much the worse for drink "
when he called.   Her sister Jean was a high trial to her
because she was given to taking drugs.   She notes a few
public events, such as the execution of Burke, the murderer,
but her entries are generally concerned with her various
friendships and domestic trials.   There appears to have been
a happy interval while Margaret was keeping a school at
Fochabers under the patronage of the Duchess of Gordon.
But for the most part her morbidity has the upper hand
throughout the diary and towards the end she gloomily
refers to herself as a poor friendless creature.   The clear
handwriting becomes shaky and confused and the diary ends
abruptly in the middle of a sentence.   Nothing can be more
pathetic than the faithful record of a drab and uneventful
life nor is there any other means of approaching so closely
to a human being.

Dr.   There is a very curious parallel in the two poisoners,
Pritchard Palmer [1] and Pritchard.   They both studied medicine, they
both poisoned their wives (among other victims), and they
both kept diaries.   Dr. Pritchard, who lived in Glasgow,
was an even more scandalous and monstrous humbug than
Palmer.   He kept two diaries, in which he records the death
of his mother-in-law, whom he also poisoned, as well as that
of his wife in 1865.   In " Letts's Medical Diary " the entries
on the occasions mentioned are very brief.

1 a.m.   Died here Jane Taylor.

Buried Mrs Taylor, poor dear Grandma, in Grange Cemetery.

Mary Jane my beloved passed away.

---

[1] *More English Diaries*, p. 29.

In "Blackwood's Shilling Scribbling Diary" there is a longer account of Mrs. Taylor's death with details—entirely false—of the medicine he prescribed for her. His wife's death is recorded thus :

Died here at 1 a.m. Mary Jane my own beloved wife aged 38 years—no torment surrounded her bedside but like a calm peaceful lamb of God—passed Minnie away.
My God and Jesus Holy Gh, one in three—welcome.
Minnie Prayer on prayer till mine be o'er ; everlasting love. Save us Lord for Thy dear Son.

The unfortunate woman had been in agonies for weeks under his slow poison. Mrs. Taylor arrived to be with her daughter, so Dr. Pritchard despatched the mother first. It will be remembered that after making a sham confession, he made a complete confession of his crimes before he was hanged, keeping up the sanctimonious note to the last. As in the case of Palmer, these diary entries were purposely used to mislead.

MINOR IRISH DIARIES

Fewer early diaries are available in Ireland. The disciplinary habit imposed by Covenanters and Puritans hardly reached there. My Irish diaries, indeed, are for the most part written by "settlers" in Ireland. Of genuine early native productions written in Irish there appear to be few, if any.

Sir Roger Wilbraham,[1] who was Solicitor-General in Ireland and Master of Requests, kept what is called a Journal between 1593 and 1616. But it never takes the form of a private diary. Political and legal matters are noted and a few anecdotes and aphorisms are introduced. He describes the dissolution of Parliament, the death of Queen Elizabeth and the Lord Chancellor's speech on the Gunpowder Plot. Sir Roger Wilbraham

O'Mellan's Journal[2] of events in Ireland in 1641–7 relates chiefly to the events in which the O'Neills were concerned. It was written in Irish and has been translated. There is O'Mellan's Journal

---

[1] Camden Miscellany, Vol. X.
[2] Trinity College, Dublin, MS. 1071.

also in Trinity College the manuscript diary of one month written by Dr. Joseph Stock, Bishop of Killala in 1798.

The Denny Family   The so-called " Denny Family Diary " [1] was begun by Sir Edward Denny, of Tralee, continued by his son, Sir Arthur, and later on by Sir Thomas in the eighteenth century.   But it is only a register of births and deaths with genealogical notes.   Sir Edward informs us :   " I finished this Great Castle and came with my mother to live in itt upon the 22 of December 1627."   It is a family register, not a diary.

James Ryan   A curious diary by James Ryan,[2] a land surveyor of Carrick-on-Suir, 1787–1809, is not kept according to dates but under subject headings.   Deaths, births, removals, accidents, etc.

William King   William King, who died in 1729 as Archbishop of Dublin, was imprisoned in 1689 when he was Dean of St. Patrick's owing to his open espousal of the cause of the Prince of Orange.   While in prison he kept a daily diary,[3] the greater part of which has survived.   Unfortunately it does not consist of any personal reflections, but gives daily reference to the rumours with regard to the exciting events outside which culminated in the battle of the Boyne and King's liberation, and he gives some account of his talks with visitors.

Charles Jasbrough   A small notebook sent to me containing a brief diary written by a certain Charles Jasbrough seemed at first hopeful, as it was very clearly written, although dated as long ago as 1726.   But on examination it turned out only to be an account of litigation and disputes with regard to the collection of tithes at Congue in Ireland, and except for a few pages of accounts there was nothing of a personal nature in the dated entries.

Dineley and Molyneux   Thomas Dineley's [4] journal of a tour in Ireland in the reign of Charles II (illustrated by excellent sketches), and

---

[1] Printed in a paper by the Rev. H. Ll. Denny.
[2] Papers in Waterford and S.E. of Ireland Archæological Society, by the Rev. P. Power.
[3] *Journal of the Royal Society of Antiquaries of Ireland.*
[4] *Kilkenny Archæological Journal,* Vol. 6, 1867.

Dr. Thomas Molyneux's diary [1] of 1709 are both exclusively
descriptive and topographical.

Sometimes one finds a tantalizing reference to diaries
which have been destroyed. For instance, in Grattan's *Life*
by his son reference is made to the diary of John, first Earl
of Clonmell, which was destroyed before his death, presum-
ably on account of the revelations as to Government methods
which it contained. Lord Clonmell

The very varied activities of John Kennedy, Presbyterian
Minister of Benburb, in Co. Down, are noted very briefly in
a diary he kept between 1724 and 1730.[2] In addition to
his duties as minister, he notes that he " thatched ye corn
and crowned ye hay rick," " put in ye hay," " sowed pasneps,"
" clean'd some seed corn," " set boxwood and cherrys,"
" put out dung," " set out potatoes," " sow'd flax," etc.,
and there are short notes about purchases, health and weather.
He seems to have been as much a farm labourer as a pastor.
He notes at the beginning that he has been lecturing on the
Psalms for seven years. John Kennedy

The journal of our first Ambassador to China [3] is entertaining. George Earl of Macartney was born in 1737 in
Co. Antrim. His journey to China took place in 1792 to
1794. He kept a daily record of the voyage and of all the
incidents culminating in his reception by the Emperor of
China. It is little more than an elaborate description of
entertainment and ceremonial, but it is written with a fullness and accuracy of detail which makes a reader share the
suppressed excitement gradually leading up to the moment
when the emperor is seen face to face.   It has in it an element
of the fantastic, like a fairy tale. Lord Macart- ney

I was very much attracted by the travel diary of an anonymous Irish clergyman [4] who visited England in 1761 and
has a lively style of writing.   There is a full description of
his crossing to England, in the course of which he writes : Anony- mous Irish Clergy- man.

I heard my fellow travellers who were still pumping and pulling

[1] *Miscellany of Irish Archæological Society*, 1846.
[2] Quoted in *Two Centuries of Life in Co. Down*, by John Stevenson.
[3] *Our First Ambassador to China*, by Helen H. Robins, 1908.
[4] British Museum, MSS. 27951.

up their Livers & Lights. Thro' pity to their weakness I made
y^m a Pott of Mr. Wainwright's tea very comfortable to troubled
Bowels. This went down glibly enough tho' they ed not swallow a
morsell of anything solid. Poor Burgess thought he shd die ere he
c^d reach ye shore and Mr. Slinter ye Actor wd have willingly quitted
all his Right and Title to ye green rooms of Both Kingdoms for one
single Inch of Terra firma.

After his visit to Westminster Abbey, he writes :

Fatigued a Little wth yesterday's expedition and conversing more
wth ye Dead than with ye living I Indulged myself this morning
wth a Nap extraordinary.

He describes a Green Park coffee-house :

Indeed I must confess this was a most Droll & diverting scene.
In one corner of ye Room you saw a man sitting solitary and overhear^g
ye chatt of others.   In another 2 or 3 citizens comfortably sitting &
smok^g their pipes.   Here were placed as many gentlemen at a Bow
window eating oysters and drinking plan Bubb And there Stephenson
ye Blinkard ye Braggadocio Bruiser & Boxer swilling Claret of 5
sh^rs a Bottle wth a companion seemingly dead Drunk whilst he was
abusing al ye world and damning ye eyes of Dukes Marquses Earls,
Lords and Knights of every order both in Church and State. As
this was a scene altogether New I was resolved to stay it out.

Most of the diary, however, is devoted only to descriptions
of sightseeing.   It would seem to have been written for
some one to read immediately, as he appears to be address-
ing some one when he says : " this depression shal not detain
me from Acquaint^g you y^t " etc.   This anonymous clergyman certainly had a talent for diary writing.

Anne
Countess
of Roden

A diary of attempted self-discipline and mild self-reproach
was kept by Anne Countess Dowager of Roden (1797–1802).[1]
She was the daughter and heiress of James Earl of Clanbrassil.
An effort to be punctual in her daily records leads to a number
of entries such as " I spent the day as usual," " I think I
was at prayers," " I can't recollect."   But she reproves herself
for them and explains her motive in keeping a diary :

These foolish little notes of the occurrences of each day are no
further use than as they help my memory ; but it is my reflections
upon my own conduct that are to be of use to me, and the considera-

---

[1] Quoted in *Two Centuries of Life in Co. Down*, by John Stevenson.

tion of how I fulfil the duties of each day, and how unworthy I am
of the hourly mercies I receive.

She deplores her faults of temper, her " neglect of retro-
spection," her " peevishness " and " irresolution " and confesses to a fault with which many will sympathize when she
writes : " I have endeavoured to bear affliction and yet sink
under vexation and am conquered by it." She was right,
vexation is a far more severe test than affliction. There is
no heroism connected with the conquest.

In 1789 she gives a detailed account of her flight to Scotland in the days of the Rebellion. In this, however, she
fails to convey alarm to the reader, although she tells us she
feels it herself. It is not every one who can stir us by the
story of an adventure.

A high place in travel diaries should be given to Miss Catherine Wilmot
Catherine Wilmot's account of her tour on the Continent
with Lord and Lady Mount Cashell, 1801–3.[1] On the fly-
leaf of the volume she wrote : " I will every now and then
record the events of the day so that like a snail wherever I
crawl I may be known by the trail I shall leave smeared
behind me in this book." There are occasional dates, but
it forms a more or less consecutive narrative addressed to
her brother Robert Wilmot.

Written in true diary form and amusingly observant is John Mayne
the Journal of John Mayne,[2] who when he was twenty-three
visited the Continent for a couple of years after the fall of
Napoleon. It is, however, objective travel observations.

Mrs. Calvert, the daughter of Lord Pery, sometime speaker Mrs. Calvert
of the Irish House of Commons, kept a diary from 1804 till
the end of her life (1859), and she reached ninety-two years
of age. Many extracts are given in a volume entitled, *An
Irish Beauty of the Regency*,[3] but they contain little more
than social gossip and superficial politics of a kind of which
we have had instances enough.

[1] *An Irish Peer on the Continent*, related by Catherine Wilmot,
ed. by Thomas Sadlier, M.A., 1920.
[2] *The Journal of John Mayne*, ed. by John Mayne, Colles, 1909.
[3] By Mrs. Warrenne Blake, 1911.

William
Alling-
ham

One is tempted to quote at length from William Allingham's diary, for there are many accounts of conversations
with Carlyle, Tennyson and other celebrities.   Himself a poet,
he came into close relationship with cther poets.   But like
Crabb Robinson, his jottings about these great men lack the
quality which makes one pay special attention and they
amount to little more than superficial gossip.   Had he com-
pleted his original intention of writing his autobiography, he
would no doubt have worked up his diary notes into a general
critical survey of the men, their characters, their habits and
their works.   But no amount of anecdote in a diary makes
up for the absence of the author's own thoughts, reflections
and doings.   Allingham's beginning of an autobiography
only gives an account of his childhood at Ballyshannon, Co.
Donegal, where he was born.   He never continued it.   The
diaries cover a long period from 1847 to 1888.   But as one
reads them the impression grows that they are notes kept
for future use in an autobiography and they really amount
to nothing more than the small talk of great people.   He
evidently read them over, for he says in a memorandum :
" I care for my old diaries for the sake of the past."   Ford
Madox Brown,[1] who lived at about the same period, also
associated with celebrated artists, but in his diary he very
properly wrote chiefly about himself.   That is what we want
—something which no one else can tell us.   The more a
diarist does that, no matter what be his nationality, his
religion, his profession or his position, the more shall we
enjoy reading his record.

[1] *More English Diaries*, p. 226.

LIST OF SCOTTISH DIARIES
ARRANGED IN CHRONOLOGICAL ORDER

Name of Diarist.	Occupation.	Date of Diary.	Source.	Page.
James Melville.	Scottish Reformer	1571–1610	*Autobiography and Diary of Mr. James Melvill.* Wodrow Saciety, 1842.	27
Archibald Johnston (Lord Wariston)	Statesman	1632–1639 1650–1654	Scottish History Society, Vol. XI (1911), and second series, Vol. XVIII (1919).	34
Sir Thomas Hope	Lord Advocate	1633–1646	*The Diary of Sir Thomas Hope,* Bannatyne Club, 1843.	41
Alexander Brodie	Lord of Sessions and Member of Parliament	1652–1680	Spalding Club, 33, 1863.	45
James Brodie .	—	1680–1685		
William Cunningham	Master of Craigends	1673–1680	Scottish History Society, Vol. II, 1887.	52
Patrick, 1st Earl of Strathmore	Lord of Sessions	1684–1689	*The Book of Record of Patrick 1st Earl of Strathmore,* Scottish History Society, vol. for 1890.	55
George Ridpath	Minister . .	1755–1761	Scottish History Society, 3° series, Vol. II, 1922.	60
Marjorie Flemming	—	1809–1811	*The Story of Pet Marjorie,* by L. Macbean, 1904. *Horæ Subsecivæ,* by Dr. John Brown, 1832.	67
Sir Walter Scott	Poet and Novelist	1825–1832	*Journal of Sir Walter Scott,* 1890, 2 vols.	74
Jane Cameron . Mrs. Mawson .		1829–1842	Memoir privately printed, 1846.	87

Name of Diarist.	Occupation.	Date of Diary.	Source.	Page.
Anne Chalmers. Mrs. Hanna .		1830	*Letters and Journals of Anne Chalmers*, ed. by her daughter, 1923.	90
Lord Cockburn.	Judge . . .	1831–1854	*Lord Cockburn's Journals*, 2 vols., 1874.	100
Jane Welsh Carlyle	—	1855–1856	*Letters and Memorials of Jane Welsh Carlyle*, Vol. II, ed. by J. A. Froude. *Reminiscences*, by Thomas Carlyle, Vol. II, ed. by J. A. Froude.	94
Samuel Cameron	Minister . .	*circ.* 1860–1872	Original manuscript in the possession of Miss Amy H. Cameron, of Edinburgh.	103

SCOTTISH DIARIES

JAMES MELVILLE

A MONGST still existing diaries of the sixteenth century there are few in which the regular daily entry is yet adopted. We find accounts and chronological notes of public events. Diary writing as a religious disciplinary exercise does not appear in its fully developed form till the succeeding century. In these early diaries, however, while the form and method may still be undeveloped, the character of the record depends as at all times on the personality of the writer.

One would hardly expect to find in the Diary of a sixteenth-century Scottish Reformer immersed all his life in ecclesiastical dispute anything more than a stiff, dry argumentative treatise on the various phases of Church controversy. But James Melville, whose diary, apart from Robert Birrell's record of public events, is the earliest existing Scottish diary, had remarkable powers of vivid narrative. The large volume, which contains immense disquisitions, notes, memoranda, declarations, etc., on the Church affairs of his time might well be supposed to daunt any but keen students of Scottish ecclesiastical history. But Melville's vigorous, fresh, telling style of writing, his descriptive powers, his introduction of picturesque episodes and more personal touches, his reporting of verbatim dialogue at the appropriate moment, and his abstention from passages of self-condemnation, which grew into a wearisome habit with his successors, come as a surprise and make this early diary one of the most engaging in the Scottish collection. He always summarizes the year, sometimes the episodes of a month, and occasionally the actual transactions of a day.

A word about the career of the man who shows his character to us so clearly in his writing. James Melville was a nephew

27

of Andrew Melville, Principal of the University of Glasgow, and subsequently of St. Andrews, and was born in 1556. He became a lecturer under his uncle in both these universities. Uncle and nephew suffered exile for their opposition to the episcopal schemes of James VI (afterwards James I of England). James Melville returned to Scotland after the taking of Stirling Castle in 1585, and in 1589 he became Moderator of the General Assembly and took an active part in Church controversy. He was summoned to London in 1606 with his uncle for the discussion of Church policy. Andrew was sent to the Tower ; James was detained near Newcastle. He died at Berwick in 1614.

The manuscript (in the Advocates Library) consists of an autobiography giving his early life, and under the headings of each year gradually slips into the form of contemporary notes or diary entries. There is a second part covering the period for 1596 to 1610 entitled, " a true narratioune of the dedyneing aige of the Kirk of Scotland," which is mostly objective historical narrative.

James Melville's diary is by no means easy to read for an Englishman. But it would be desecration to translate into insipid modern English the extracts from this diary in which the spelling and language seem almost to give us the sound of his voice. Careful reading out loud with due regard to the Scottish accent helps to solve many of the spelling puzzles. While of course he gives chief attention to his lively interest in Church matters, he does not omit domestic details. For instance, he records that in 1586 when he experienced " great fascherie and vexation " " a comfortable benefit " was bestowed on him by God " in the middes thairof ; to wit, of a pleasand second sone."

He is never content with just reporting baldly the King's visit or his conferences. He gives a full account making the King speak. In 1587 King James visited St. Andrews, where Melville's uncle " Mr. Andro " was Principal.

About the end of Junie, his Majestie cam to St Androis, and brought with him the said Du Bartas, and coming first without anie warning to the New Collage, he calles for Mr. Andro, saying he was com with that gentleman to haiff a Lessone. Mr. Andro answeres,

That he haid teatched his ordinar that day in the fornoone. " That is all ane," sayes the King, " I mon haiff [1] a lessone, and be heir within an houre for that effect." And, indeid, within les nor an houre, his Majestie was in the scholl, and the haill Universitie convenit with him ; befor whom Mr. Andro extempore intreated maist cleirlie and mightelie of the right government of Chryst, and in effect refuted the haill Actes of Parliament maid against the discipline thairof, to the grait instruction and confort of his auditor, except the King allean,[2] wha was verie angrie all that night.

Another talk with the King :

Upon the morn, befor Assemblie tyme, I was commandit to com to the King, and Mr. Andro withe me ; wha, entering in his Cabinet, began to dell verie fearlie [3] with my uncle ; bot thairefter entering to twitche maters, Mr. Andro brak out with his wounted humor of fredome and zeall, and ther they hecled on till all the hous, and clos, bathe hard, mikle of a large houre. In end, the King takes upe and dismisses him favourablie.

" Mr. Andro " gets the King in a corner on another occasion so that His Majesty is obliged to evade the issue and laugh it off :

the King was fean to tak it upe betwixt tham with gentill termes and mirrie talk ; saying " They war bathe little men, and thair hart was at thair mouthe."

The final conference in 1606 is elaborately described day by day. In an ordinary diary we should not be attracted by this sort of recital nor would there be anything to comment on beyond the objective facts. But James Melville gives an atmosphere which makes one, in spite of the difficulties of his spelling and language, read on. We see the King while the others are talking reading over the papers with " ane angry smyle " ; we are told that some of Melville's colleagues spoke their mind " most friely, statly (stoutly) and plainely to the admiratioun of the English auditorie, quho wer not accustomit to heir the King so talkit to and reassonit with," and we have the King losing his temper and breaking into oaths and finally " cuttitly ryseing and turneing his back, he sayes " God be with you, Siris ! "

---

[1] Must have.   [2] Alone.   [3] Fairly, smoothly.

In an earlier part of the diary he gives an excellent description of John Knox :

with a furring of martriks [1] about his neck, a staff in the an hand, and guid godlie Richart Ballanden, his servand, halding upe the uther oxtar,[2] from the Abbay to the paroche kirk ; and be the said Richart and another servant, lifted upe to the pulpit, whar he behovit to lean at his first entrie ; bot or he haid done with his sermont, he was sa active and vigorus that he was lyk to ding that pulpit in blads, and fly out of it !

The account he gives of a fanatical preacher taking advantage of an interval before the acting of a play to the King at Dundee is particularly good :

Whar, on a day, the gentilmen of the countrey about haid a gyse [3] and farce to play befor the King ; His Majestie was in the new Innes of the Abay, befor the windowes wharof the schow was to be maid. Grait confluence of peiple conveined, and the place read with a fear circuit ; It continowed void for the space of a lang houre, wither that his Majestie was nocht readie to behauld, or the playars to present tham selves, I can nocht tell, bot, whill all ar gasing and langing for the play, in stappes Schipper Lindsay, a knawin frenetic man,[4] and paesses upe and down in the circuit with a grait gravetie, his hands in his syde, looking verie big and hiche.[5]   The man was of a grait telyie,[6] weill bigged,[7] of a large face, and guid manlie countenance, all rouche [8] with heire, his browes grait tuftes of heire, and als grait a tuft upon the verie neb of his nease [9] ; his look was verie reasit [10] and hiche : Wherat first the peiple maid a noyse with lauching ; bot when he began to speak, he movit sic attention as it haid bein to a preatcher ; and, indeed, for my part, I was mair movit with it then with monie preatchings.

He goes on to describe the discourse and the effect it had on the Earl of Morton who stood in the " boss windo " " gnapping [11] on his staff end." He was " mikle movit with this first interlude, as ernest and nocht play ; sa, that during all the sportes that followed, he altered never the gravitie of his countenance."

[1] Marten.   [2] Armpit.
[3] Masquerade.   [4] A known madman.
[5] High.   [6] Stature.
[7] Built.   [8] Rough.
[9] Point of his nose.   [10] Raised, i.e., angry.
              [11] Gnawing.

His travelling adventures are described. On one occasion in an open boat all on board had to take turns at rowing :

na man was ydle, yea, I rowit my selff, till the hyd cam af my fingars, mair acquented with the pen nor working on an are (oar).

He records also a fall from a horse :

This yeir, ryding upe to Carnbie, in companie with the Lard of Balfour and his brother, to desing the manse and gleib of the Kirk to Mr. Andro Hounter, minister, upon an kitle [1] hat ridden hors, approtching to a strype [2] weill how of sevin or aught feet brod, I put at the hors to cause him lope [3] it ; and because he was evill-mouthed and hat ridden, I held his head streat, wharat he repyning in the middes of his lope, cust down his head, sa that all the seddle-gear braking, he cust me ower on the uther bank with the sedle betwix my legges, and his heid going down, he lopes the supersault, and his buttokes lightes hard besyd me, with all his four feit to the lift ! [4] The lyk wharof was never hard in the judgment of the behaulders, and all that hathe considderit it sen syne, without anie hurt to man or beist, except the sadle-grathe braking.

There are several references to " the sweit tender-harted young las," his wife. Of the birth of his son Ephraim in England he gives a graphic description :

My wyff was at the sam tyme grait with chyld, neir hir birthe, and, heiring of Mr. James' deathe, wha, by the comoun and publict respect, was to hir in affection a father, brought upe daylie in his hous and companie with his wyff, sche doollit and bursted sa,[5] I being in Newcastell with the Lords, that they war all in grait fear sche sould haiff parted with her birthe. Amangs whom, a godlie suddart, (named Francis Goodwin) comforting hir, sayes, " Tak heid what yow do, Mistres Melvin, that yow becom nocht an unnaturall murderar of that quhilk is in your bellie, quhilk by appeirance is a man chyld ; and yow knaw nocht if God may mak him to supplie a place in his Churche againe ! " Within a monethe thairefter sche was lichtar of a man chyld indeid, whom, be imitation of Josephe, I callit Ephraim, because God haid maid me fruictfull in a strange land ; praying God of his grace, nocht regarding my sinnes and unthankfulnes, to mak anie mean instrument in his Kirk. I can nocht expres the cair, kyndnes, and tender affection quhilk God kindlit in the harts of that peiple towards me, in the bahalff of my wyff and chyld ; For, certean I am, if all hir frinds and myn in Scot-

---

[1] Ticklish.   [2] Stream.   [3] Leap.   [4] Sky.
[5] Mourned and sobbed in such a manner.

land haid bein about hir, it was nocht in thair power to haiff used hir sa cairfullie, lovinglie, tenderlie, and diligatlei ; [1] and, namlie I war maist ingrat if I sould forget my guid, godlie, and maist courteus Lady, my Lady Wedringhton, wha wated on mair cairfullie then the maidwyff, and receavit him from the wombe in hir awin skirt, and finding him nocht livlie, maid hast to the fyre, and thrusting in her curshar,[2] brunt it, and helde to his naisthrilles, wherby he quicned and kythed [3] signes of lyff.   This I sa particularlie sett down, partlie till extoll the cair and providence of God towards me, and partlie to move that chyld to sett him selff to the knawlage and service of that God wha thus brought him from the wombe.   He was born the 15 day of Januar, in the yeir 1584–(1585).

The death of his son Andro, who was " beautifull, loving and mirrhie," is accompanied by an incident which he describes :

I can nocht forget a strange thing at his deathe.   I haid a pear of fyne milk whait dowes [4] quhilk I fed in the hous : The ane wharof that day of his deathe could nocht be haldin af his cradle, bot stopped from sitting about it, crape in and sitt in under it, and died with him : The uther, at my hamcoming on the morn, as I was washing my hands, cam, lighted at my futt, and pitiuslie crying, " Pipe, pipe, pipe ! " ran a little away from me.   Then I called for peyes and beanes to giff it ; bot they schew me it wald nocht eatt.   I tuk it upe, and put pikles in the mouthe bot it schuk tham out of the throt ; and parting from me with a pitifull piping, within twa or thrie houre died also.

He composes some verses on the doves and under them he writes :

This page, if thou be a pater that reids it, thow wilt apardone me. If nocht suspend thy censure till thow be a father, as said the grave Lacedomonian, Agesilaus.

This looks as if James Melville expected an eventual reader of his record.   He often breaks into poetry and after the murder of his friend James Smithe he finds his " poeticall passion " gives him some relief, although he apologizes for the poem, saying it is

bot a dwabbling countrey ryme, meittar to be swipped away with the mouse-wobbes (cobwebs) nor byd as a picture in the palace of Apollo.

---

[1] Delicately.   [2] Kerchief.   [3] Manifested.
[4] A pair of fine milk-white pigeons.

Those who have to study Scottish Church history are fortunate in having this period presented to them with, possibly strong bias, but undoubtedly a freshness and liveliness of style which gives human interest to the dry bones of controversy.

The Diary was published in full in 1842 by the Wodrow Society, edited by Robert Pitcairn.

ARCHIBALD JOHNSTON
(LORD WARISTON)

FOR the information of those who live south of the Tweed it may be necessary to say a word about the career of Archibald Johnston, Lord Wariston. He was one of the most remarkable of leading Scotsmen in the mid-seventeenth century. He assisted in framing the Scots National Covenant in 1638 ; he was made a Lord of Sessions in 1641. He took a prominent part in the Westminster Assembly and became one of the committee representing Scotland in London. Subsequently he was made Lord Advocate and Lord Clerk Register. He was supposed to have given the fatal advice to Lesley which led to the defeat of the Scots before Cromwell at Dunbar. He lost his offices, but as a leading " remonstrant " he was renamed by Cromwell and sat in the House of Lords during the Protectorate. At the Restoration he was arrested at Rouen and after being tried by the Scottish Parliament was hanged at Edinburgh. This is only a very bare outline and in no way covers the many political activities of this notable Scottish figure.

Carlyle, who had only read his letters, refers to him as " a canny lynx-eyed Lawyer and austere Presbyterian Zealot ; full of fire of heavy energy and of gloom."

Although it was well known that Wariston kept a diary, it was not till about thirty years ago that any traces of it were found and then only a fragment. The discovery of a considerable portion of it only occurred in 1906 when Lord Binning called attention to numerous manuscript volumes in his library at Mellerstein. With several gaps the Diary has now been published in two sections, 1632 to 1639 and 1650 to 1654. Wariston was as regular a diarist as anyone mentioned in these volumes. He wrote every day, often covering a large number of pages. With all the advantages of a clearly printed page before us, we must confess that this portentous document is heavy reading, not only because it is written in lowland Scotch, which for the more ignorant necessitates an occasional glance at the glossary, but because his severity and his gloom are extremely oppressive. Many English examples have been given of diarists who were continually overcome by their own sinfulness, but this Scot takes the lead of them all. A very large proportion of his entries are devoted to prayer and imprecation. He supplicates, adjures, argues with and even scolds the Almighty, often with great violence of language, and in one passage challenges Jesus Christ to go before His Father and plead for him. His devotions and the sermons he listens to occupy a large amount of space. Although colloquially expressed, the descriptions of his political activities are very difficult to follow, but now and again there is a little relief in his references to domestic affairs. Wariston attached great importance to his Diaries and he asks his Lord to

preserve this diary out of His enemyes' hands and sanctifye them for the glorye of His ane nayme and the good of His people and especyaly of my childrein for whom they ar written.

His motive is therefore clear, and he certainly cultivated the habit to the fullest degree.

Wariston enjoyed gloom. He revelled in gloom. His repentances are real orgies. He refers to himself in one of his supplications to God as

Thy poore, naughty, wretched, unuseful, passionat, humerous, vayne, proud, silly, imprudent, phantastick barroman,

and in another as :

the unworthyest, fillthiest, passionatest, deceitfullest, crookedest, backslydingest, rebellionest, perjurest, unaiblest of all his servants.

It was unnecessary to say more. In his prayers there is no sort of moderation. They always appear to be the occasion for an attack of frenzy. His " soule schouts in extreme bitterness." In thinking of a text in the middle of the night he is moved " unto sorrowe and tears in sutche a degree as my verrie heart failed me." He has "innumerable tears and unexpressable sighs." He begins "to youle, mourne and lament with many tears to my great contentment." His soul " out of unspeakable bitterness schouted for and invited sorrow, grief, tears, comfortlessness, heartlesnes, solitarines, melancholy for to come and duell with me." He is " moved by the sight of my natural corruption." His tears are sometimes " publick tears," sometimes " tears in my eyes " or his heart is " bursted with many floods of con-juring tears " and sometimes he is " melted into tears within my. bowels." It would seem they were actual not figurative tears when he tells us he prayed

in Wariston gallerie for One hour and one half with great abundance of continual guschings of tears and with frequent sudaine motions."

He must have had what the French call " la larme facile."

The first section of the Diary is entitled *Memento Quamdiu Vivas*. The early part of it is retrospective. Each section is addressed to his soul in the vocative " O Saule remember " or " O Saule never forget " or " Heir, saule, remarque," etc., until he settles down to his regular daily entries.

In 1632 Wariston, who was then twenty-one, married Jean Stewart, who was " ane bairn " not yet fourteen years old. " Al hir freinds and thy freinds, yea all indifferent persons hearing of it, thought it the fittest matche that ever was in Edinbrugh." Jean was said to be " haistie and kankard " and her face " was al spoiled by the poks." Wariston was not enthusiastic at first. On the morning of the wedding they made a paction with each other, he " promising never to gloume nor glundre on hir befor folks and schoe never to disobey in any compagnie." On the following Sunday morn-ing while they were in bed, he examined her on her knowledge of God, and his heart was " ravisched with hir ansuears and blessed God for hir." At Communion her eyes were " like rae collops [1] for greating " and to him " her bludered face seiemed then most beautiful." The poor little child wife, however, died in the following year and Wariston was for

[1] Pieces of roedeer flesh.

months inconsolable. He " roared," " youled pitifully " and
" skirled " for pardon.

His health and diet are subjects of his concern always
from the spiritual point of view, as the following extracts
show :

Upon Tuesday night I eated flesch, contraire to my custom of
fasting becaus that dyet keaped me from night's rest, dryed up my
body and filled my brain with phantasies, and by wakening the hot
bilious and dust melancholik humeurs, subjected my body most to
thos sam tentations quhilk I stryved to escheu be fasting.

Al this tyme I fand my stomak wambling within me every morning
and my heart inclyning to seaknes ; even the Lords will be doone,
wealcome is his pleasure quehensover it cometh.

This afternoone I took a great sleepynesse and payne of my head
and quasinesse of my stomak and grew affrayed of the sixes and so
did my wyfe.

This was his second wife, Helen Hay, a daughter of Lord
Foresterseat, whom he married in 1634, having warned her
of his " imperfections of cankardnes, sillines, and profaines,
to the end shoe might be forwarned of the hazard.' Judging
by his references to her she must have been a woman of great
character and ability, as she participates in many of his
political activities, interviewing Cromwell, Colonel Fenwick
and the English judges and writing letters to him of advice
and information. But Wariston's estate had rapidly dimin-
ished owing to his carelessness in money matters and Helen
had so hard a time that it affected her health :

I remembered hou my wyfes seaknes was thought to proceid from
melancholy for the daylie decay of my stait. This I represented to
God as a great strait both to haive my estait to melt away quhen
I expected with submission upon his promise for the increase of it
and to losse my wyfe for the grief of that decay.

I told hir my conception of hir seaknesse as a correction for hir
neglect of secret worship and wayring hir strength and health on
uther busines preferred to that, which therefor God blasted becaus
of not petitioning to Himself.

I found my wyfe mightily mooved to teares and groanes which
maid me insist the mor on sutes for mercy and grace ; and shoe went

to hir bed and I found hir oppressed with greife. I found . . . that shoe aprehended I and my familye was ruyned in my estate ; and shoe wished to be out of the world as on cause of it as shoe sayed.

I found my wyfe very cankered about our affaires and wishing rayther to be a servant to any then the burthensom lyfe shoe had and the litle ease or help shoe had from me. This mynded me of my unserviceablenesse to God and unusefulnesse to my awen, and unpleasantnesse to myself and hatefulnesse at hom and abroad.

He has a "distemper" at her spending the day "on vanityes and worldly business" and he speaks his mind "sharply" to her and to his daughter "for ther promiscuous dancing at the mariage." But he records that she sold her "sylver-work to interteane his familye" and that a servant girl left because she did wear her clothes so long and made them up again for her children, so there was no chance of the girl getting them.

Wariston must have been a difficult man to live with. At the end his poor wife lived to experience the horror of her husband's capture and trial and of his death by hanging at the Market Cross of Edinburgh under the windows of the house which for many years had been their Edinburgh home.

A candid friend tells him on one occasion of some of his curious habits :

He then told of folks observing in the kirk my wrything at the psalmes, my wagging my head and weavling my mouth in the singing and that it was offensive ; and if I did not wrythe in the tyme of privat singing no mor should I doe in publick singing.

Wariston is fond of recording his dreams and also his wife's dreams and there are many passages which show his superstitious nature.

It would require a pretty full knowledge of the Scottish history of the period and of the part played by Wariston in it to be able to follow intelligently his account of his public activities. A diarist's history written day by day is always awkward to mould together into the more concise form in which historians represent the events in after years. Moreover, his style is difficult and the incessant habit of breaking off at a tangent to have an altercation with or supplication to the Almighty makes the sequence of events still more confusing. But we can recognize the irreconcilable nature of the rigid Covenanter who in Council and committee was always " free " in his speech and ready with a text to reinforce his argument. We can read not only of his legal career but of his dealings with the King and with the Army in war time. In his interviews with Cromwell when the latter was " passionate and hauty " Wariston writes : " I of purpose eshuned heate." He had learned he was more likely to get what he wanted if he kept his temper. But as we are not concerned with the history but with the diary, it will suffice to give a few examples of his recital of his public duties and political events. Here is his account of the introduction of the service book into Scotland in 1637 :

Upon Sunday the tuentie thrid of July that blak doolful Sunday to the Kirk and Kingdome of Scotland the service book beyond to be read in the Kirk and Kingdome of Scotland. At the beginning thairof thair rayse sik a tumult, sik ane outcrying quhat both peoples murmuring, mourning, rayling, stool-casting, as the lyk was never scein in Scotland ; the bischop both after the foranoones sermon was trampled under foot and afternoone being coatched with Roxburgh was almost stoned to death ; the dean was forced to caige himself in the steeple.

Then follows at great length his own views on " this spiritual plauge of Æigiptian darknes."

Here is an extract from his very detailed account of his doings with the army in 1650 :

I heard from Cochran and Ballantin that the Inglish sayd no grace before and after meat, had no sermons on Sunday, had a strange confidence of victory, desyred no mor bot us to feyght with them ; that Cromwell sayd he was asseurd of victory as of his awen salvation, as God was in heaven, yea utherwyse that Chryst (blessed be His holy nayme) was a lyar ; that wee had Lambert prisoner and let him goe agayn, that wee destroyed mor corne than they. When I heard that they, instead of sermon, wer killing Bacleugh's dear and spoyling the countrey, I thought it God's just judgment upon us for the disorders of our airmy in Ingland upon their people. They sayd they that fell on was mad with strong drink . . . our subcommittee is dissolved becaus of som's gruging at it. . . . Cromwell intended on Mononday to have stormed our trinch, wer not Col. Monk. They look not on us as men. His bragging letter beares to meet us and what we can bring with us. I hope we can bring God with us who soon can taik order with that proud piece of day. I got two letters from my wyfe full of surmises and misreports of us hindering battel and weakning airmy by purging.   O Lord direct us.

A general entry which is both public and domestic :

Just as I was going to the familye prayer I got M. J. G. letter shewing that he had received a letter from the Protector, was dealt with much by Col. Lokhart and spok with Monk, but had no clearnesse in the call and so had written his excuse ; and that it was lyk to be on of his greatest tryels and should shortly give me a full accoumpt of it.   I blissed God for this direction of His servant. . . . I wrote afternoone to M. J. G.   I fand myself under desertion at night and after prayer my wyfe told me of the increase of hir disease and daunger thereof.   I, at my wyfe's desyre, went and lay down the staire heavye, and cryed often for mercye.

On many occasions he makes a long retrospect of events. He certainly endeavoured continually to consider his life as a whole. His careful and unusually developed diary habit shows an exceptionally self-regardant nature.

A " great book " he refers to as having been put in Edinburgh Castle was in all probability the volume which would have filled the gap of eleven years between the two sections of the diary now available.

Wariston must be placed in the front rank of diarists. His diary is not light reading, but that is due to his disposition rather than his method.   His whole character is reflected in it with perhaps a softer note owing to his private penitence than those who had any dealings with him were ever allowed to see. We cannot dislike so forceful and active a man in spite of his failure not " to gloume nor glundre," but we should have been sorry to serve on a Committee with him and still more to have lived with him.

The first volume of the Diary was issued by the Scottish History Society in 1911, edited by George Morison Paul ; the second in 1919, edited by David Hay Fleming

SIR THOMAS HOPE

B ETWEEN 1633 and 1646 Sir Thomas Hope kept memoranda of his official and private correspondence and noted public events and births and deaths. Sir Thomas was a distinguished Scottish statesman, a very successful lawyer, and a man of great independence of opinion. He upheld the cause of the Covenanters and the Marquis of Hamilton, who was Charles I's Commissioner, found him, according to Burnet, one of his greatest troubles and yet dared not dismiss him. He was appointed Lord Advocate in 1626 and Lord High Commissioner of the General Assembly in 1643. He died in 1646, the year in which the diary concludes. It has been said of him that " he defended the civil rights of the Crown whenever he thought they were in danger ; but he refused to support under any pretext the policy of forcing on the people of Scotland a system of church government which they detested." [1]

It is not, however, from his diary that we learn much of his public activities. Most of the memoranda refer to the receipt or dispatch of letters and " pacquets." Many of the notes are of this description :

sent with Captain Maxwell ane letter to the Lord Stirling desyring him to send the contract and signater of Tillicultry hither quhilk was sent him a yeir since.

Sir Thomas was evidently domestic, as he makes frequent reference to the members of his family. He had four sons, John Lord Craighill, Thomas Lord Kerse, Sir James Hope, and Alexander. Of the last he writes on many occasions.

My sone Alexander went to Court and geven him 60 lb sterling.

---

[1] *The Lord Advocates of Scotland,* by George W. T. Ormond.

Item. that my sone at Windsoir wes sworn bi his Maiestie in extraordinar Carver.

And later he becomes " ordinar Carver."

Alexander's debts and allowance occupy his attention :

This day Mr. Nathaniel Volevard his servand presentit to me a tikket to him from Mr. Alexander testifeing that he had borrowit of him only XIII. lb sterling quhilk I did instantlie pay and retene the tikket.

On one occasion he asks Alexander to buy him " a jowell " and to let him know the " bignes of the diamondis with the pryce." And Alexander gives him a " rod with the Kings Majestie's portrait on the head of it of porcupine penne." Alexander also insists on his father's portrait being painted .

This day William Jamesoun painter (at the ernest desyr of my sone Mr. Alexander) was sufferit to draw my pictur.

He always enters the birth of his grandchildren with the amount he gives to the midwife. In one case he is caused a good deal of anxiety :

About 3 efternone, my dauchter Anne Foules delyverit of a man-child blessit be the Lord ; and gevin to the midwyff j dd. angel. But the bairne was verie waik and I desyrit him to be baptizit ; quhilk my wyff excusit, that thai durst not tak the bairne forth in the cold air. And it plesit God to keip in his lyfe till Sounday at 7 hours ; and I causit him to be baptized bi Mr. Andro Ramsay in the Mag-dalen Chapell and he was namit James. And my wyff wes angrie at my griefe.

This is the only mention he makes of his wife except in the cases of letters from or to her ; but it is enough to give us some impression of her. He reports the illness in 1643 of his son Thomas, who was " very sad and melancholious," and then his death :

My deir sone departit on 23 August 1643 being Weddinsday a litill befoir 9 hours of nycht. The Lord comfort me and his poore bedfellow and supplie his and my wants and bliss his deir children.

On the occasion of the birth of a child to his daughter, Lady Cambuskynneth, there was a fire.

Item with this the Lord gave a blissing in the nicht befoir her delyverie ffor the lycht stair of my sone James, his studie tuik fyir quhilk wes espyit bi the smok arrysing and sua the Lord has vouch-saffit a doubill mercie.

But this was not nearly so serious as when his ruff took fire from a candle behind him and he could not put it out :

quhairupon I cuist my gown from me and ran down the bak passage crying for help, but gat none till I cam to the hall, quhair the servandis cam furth, and specially the steuart James Twysdaill, and glaspitt the low in his handis and tuik my ruff from my craig and so freed me off my feir, ffor quhilk I pray the Lord to mak me thankfull for it wes a greit mercie.

There are occasional notes of public events such as :

This day the Queanies Majestie delyverit of a maid child.

From time to time he makes certain resolutions or vows which are carefully noted :

This day I vowit to my Lord, humilitie, patience, abstinence, sobriete and not to eat but one kynd of meit a dinner and not above 2 drinks of wyne. The Lord give me grace to perform it.

This day renewit my vow to the Lord and addit to it, not to kyth any impatience agaiuis any injuries offerit to me but to pour them furth befoir the Lord.

In a health note he describes " a heavy brasche of the colick quhilk vexit me till I vomit all." He takes very seriously a nasty fall occasioned by his chair breaking under him when he was snuffing the candle :

This day as I wes making for reading off my ordinarie lectures off the Scripture, and colling the candill and casting the coll furth off the scheiris in the fyre, the schyre quhairin I satt coupit and I gatt ane heavy fall on my bak on the ground but my heid was saiff. Blessit be the Lord and God gif me grace to tak this for warningis that my Lord is preparing me for the last.

Sir Thomas was undoubtedly superstitious and the most curious feature of the diary, which is little more than a busi-ness record, is the way he constantly sets down his dreams, in which he sometimes hears the voice of God talking to him :

About midnycht as I was regrating to the Lord the calamitie off his Kirk and humblie praying his Majestie to arrise to the help thairoff and with teares urging, calling unto him, Arryse ! I hard thir words " I will arryse."

Lying in bed betwix 1 and 2 in the morning I wes pouring furth my hart to the Lord ; and in so gret necessitie being to speik with the King, I said " My Lord, will not thy Majestie help and assist me ? "   And I hard a voice saying " I will, doubt nott."

This nycht a dream occarit quhilk carryis some fear with it ; but I wait on the Lord.   It wes that the rod quhairwith I walk with wes broken in pieces, and nothing left of it but the silver head.

Dreamit that I tuik out one of my schaft toothes with my awin hand.   The Lord prepare me.

Dreamit that I wes at the marriage of my sone Sir Alexander with my dauchter Anna Foules ; a folische dream.

On the appearance of a meteor he says : " This portendis strange and fearfull events. The Lord make us ready."

We feel sure this eminent man of the law did not speak of his fears and premonitions publicly, but confided them probably only to his diary.   There is something peculiarly incongruous in entries of this description, coming in the midst of the dry official and business notes.

The Diary was published in 1843 by the Bannatyne Club, but unfortunately without any notes or comments.

ALEXANDER BRODIE OF BRODIE
AND HIS SON JAMES

ALTHOUGH Brodie accuses himself of " covetousness, unevenes, self love, envi, pryd, self conceit, forgetting my engagements, carelessness to honour God, unwatchfulness, declining " and condemns himself as an " unsound-harted wretch, doubl, unstable, deceitful," he never reaches Wariston's savage pitch of self-condemnation. Brodie knew Wariston and he admits : " albeit I cam not up to him in his neglect of the world, abstractednes from worldli employment, zeal, fervencie of spirit."

Brodie was just as punctual a diarist as Wariston, but a great deal of his record is lost. The part that survives begins in 1652. There are five volumes, with gaps between each. The gaps are due to the loss of the manuscript, not to Brodie's irregularity. He never failed to write even when he was in great pain, and he makes an entry on the very day of his death, April 16, 1680.

Alexander Brodie was a strict Covenanter, for some time Member of Parliament for the County of Elgin and a Lord of Sessions. He was entrusted with many important duties. But he is far more concerned in his diary, with his own " sinful craftiness " and his " bitter, tart, impatient nature " than with the public affairs in which he participated. The diary was a religious exercise, not written for publication. Yet we find the curious misgiving and usual safeguard against the prying eye which so many diarists adopt in the fact that occasionally he breaks into an undecipherable shorthand. But the shorthand is often only used for covenience. His handwriting was very bad, he used contractions freely and the deciphering of the manuscript, therefore, caused much trouble. Part of the diary was transcribed as early as 1740

45

and the full transcript of all that was available was published
by the Spalding Club in 1863.

Entry after entry contains long catalogues of his sins and
indeed no other subject tempts him to write at any length.
Not only his own sins but the sins of his family and household occupy an immense amount of space. At " the solemn
Humiliation " in 1654 the declarations of sinfulness of all
present are recorded in full. Some of the paragraphs begin
" Mr John acknowledged his predominant sins of worldliness
and earthly mindedness etc." " Old Francis renewed his
confession with tears. . . ." " David disclaimed all strength
in himself. . . ." " Janet expressed meikle distrust of herself." " The Lady Leathin dar'd promise little of herself.
. . ." " Katherine burst forth in the complaint of her
woful, sad, deserted case. . . ." And so on. Again in 1656
he assembles the family and they all make confessions of
guilt and solemn " engadgments," beginning with the Laird
of Brodie himself. Janet Fraser " that blaspheming drunken,
unclean wretch " joined with the rest. But he has to record
on the very next day that Janet " within a few hours of her
engadgment " had " broken out in execrabl passion and
violent cursing."

Hardly a day passes without his catching himself up for
some fault :

I cam to Moortoun and heard that Craigstoun had attempted to
bui or exchang his lands for Cromarti. I saw much off my own
confident, daring, ambitious, covetous natur. I did not mor piti him
then abus my self under mani such lyk thoughts.

I went to Forres and staid al night ther about Aikinway's business
and son's ther. I found myself our taken with mor liberal eating
then was fitt : so much did I indulg my sinful fleshli apetit.

With all due respect to the Laird's zeal for self-correction,
we cannot help thinking he carries it too far when he regards
even his love of trees as sinful. This is shown in the following entries :

This day I intended to plant and graft trees and was a little
employed therein. I desired to have my sinful affection pardond
in going about thes natural things.

I planted trees in the gald and on the green. Ther is a season to sow and plant which if it be neglected cannot again be recovered. Al that's planted of tre is lorch. I was lykwys snedding and planting; but oh! soe litl as I saw or discernd of the Lord in all my employment.

In going about the feilds I found the hart apt to rys with carnal delight in feilds, grass, wood, etc. This I desird the Lord to guard me against, that such decaying corruptibl poor comforts, steal not away my heart.

I was taken up inordinatlie about trash and hagg.[1] Let not the Lord imput it.

In the holly he sees an emblem of the world:

I look on the leavs of the holie tree, thoght it represented to me the beauti of the world; green was it, but full of pricks and hurt them only who did cleave most to it.

When in London he sees:

beyond Bishopsgate a varieti of trees, plants, floures. I am apt to be inordinat about thes earthli delights and to lay me down as it wer in my nest; but my thoghts ar not Thyn.

The Almighty of course is made responsible for all events both great and small. During a storm of rain, Brodie writes:

I saw how great a God He was that did hang up thes botls above and squeiz them forth upon our heads at his pleasure.

In 1661 Alexander Brodie journeyed to London on horseback. He remained there ten months, but his diary is not very illuminating during that period. He of course notes sermons and after attendance at St. Margaret's, Westminster, he writes:

I marveiled to se men in the abstract speak of the holines of God soe weil and yet in the application mistake. So natural is it to us to corrupt and mix the most pur truth and the worship of God. Yet I found litle light or tendernes about thes things.

More than once he acknowledges "I found my inclination not averse from a form of Liturgi." He associates with several Scottish noblemen, but he is not happy and moreover is ill for a while. He breaks out one day:

[1] Clearing out copses and hedging (trash = sticks of dead underwood, hagg = hedge).

My desir was to the Lord to ridd me of this place. It is a place I have noe fellowship in. 2. I am in noe particular calling. 3. I am doing noe good in it. 4. I desir to be restord to thes I am tied to for the Lords Glorie.

And he also says : " This, this shall be a humbling journey, goe things as they will." He manages, however, to see the King, although he says very little about his interview :

Yesterday, I had access to the King and kissed his hand. Now I desir to reckon this as a merci considering how men have labourd to prejudg him against me. It was mor then I almost looked for : now I lean on him all that concerns me.

After his return to Scotland, he continues his business notes, and records news he hears, and the goings and comings of his family. Although in affairs, both public and private, he laments continually the wickedness of the times, he is not without hope of the future when he says : " I beleeved that, guhen I was dead, the noonday should be seen, thogh I saw but the day break."

There are several entries which show his preoccupation about witches. He describes the meetings of " the Commissioners for witches." The witches are condemned to be burnt, although Brodie himself takes a more enlightened and broader view. " I desird not to be lookd on as the pursuer of thes poor creaturs."

Again we find Brodie taking the tolerant view in an interview with Mr. Thomas Hogg, Minister of Kiltearn, which is admirably related, and although long, must be quoted in part as indicating Brodie's character as well as anything in the diary :

Efter dinner good Mr. Th Hogg cam to me anent Alr. Chisholm ; but did fal to expostulate with me for the favours which I bear to wicked men. I desired not to speak but to hear. Yet he prest on me and I said I durst not tak on me to judg the estat of others and I thoght it might consist with a seid of grac to fall in wicked acts frequentli, of drunkenness, lying or the lyk. He, and one in the estat of grac, may be frequentli, mor than one or twic overtaken with thes sinful acts. He said, That to be frequent in wicked acts of the lyk kind he could not but judg them in the way to hell. I said, Ther action I disalloud, so did they, perchanc, themselves and wer burthend with it. But for ther failing, so I durst not cal them or reckon them amongst the wicked : grace may be smothered with much and frequent corruptions and weakneses. The holi man exprest so much indignation at my expression and opinion, and that he abhord it and that I stumbld him greatlie : my woful heart kindld and I said I did noe less dislyk his severiti in censuring the condition and estat of others and that he took the keys and judgd rashlie and rigidlie ; and that I could not embrac the opinion becaus Mr. Tho. Hogg said it, and if he stumbld at me he might forbear me. He was sorri that my children should hear such doctrin. Lord ! piti both my hastines, rashnes, and ignorance and the want of reverence to that holi man, guhem I had in great esteem ; and guherin I may be in errour the Lord discover it to me and convince and let me not go on in it, for Thy nam's sak. . . . I did afterwards cal Mr. Tho. asid and lovingli askd, why he kindld soe vehementli against me. I hopd we minded the sam thing and had the sam object of our lov and hatred albeit his was mor intens for good and against evel than min. But I desird unfeinedli to hate evel and lov good. Ani sin continued in and fallen in, without repentance condemns ; but how oft a child of God may fall, and ris, and repent, it is hard to define.

In fact, Brodie was far more tolerant than most of his generation, and was in himself more human than the outpourings in his diary would lead us to suppose. He was not above taking " over great liberti in eating and drinking " and he even " made use of golfing for exercis of the body " without asking for God's forgiveness.

Towards the end, when he is "in great distress and heavines," one can feel the effort of his continued writing. Notwithstanding the recurrence of painful symptoms, which he describes, he goes on to the day of his death, on which the entry runs :

I heard read Job 15. 20 " The wicked man travels with pain all his days and the number of years is hid to the oppressour."

There is something rather fine in the stalwart old Covenanter's ceaseless endeavour to live up to his high ideal and his determination not to judge too harshly his fellow-men. It was to his diary privately, we feel sure, and not to his friends publicly, that he made these full and exhaustive confessions and carried on his combat with " Satan—that old crooked serpent." With his judicial mind and philosophic outlook, occupied with his many duties and giving sound advice to his friends, loving trees and flowers and " taken

4

up inordinatlie about trash and hagg," Alexander Brodie
was no doubt a much respected and lovable man.

The pen as it falls from the hand of Alexander is immediately taken up by James, his son, who had been taught to
follow his father's example in this respect.   In 1653 we read
in the father's diary :

> My Son (after acknowledgment and conviction of meikle unfaith-
> fulness and unsoundness and hollow heartedness in following the
> Lord according to his engagement and covenant) did after confession
> to the Lord's glory, seek mercy, and renew the covenant betwixt the
> Lord and his soul.   This is written in my first Diary book, likeas it
> is in my Son's Diary which he is to begin.

When Alexander dies James proceeds the very next day
to give a full account of his father's death and afterwards
of his funeral.   He writes :

> I desire to be troubld that ever in word or thoght I offended my dear
> Father, that I have not made that use of his companie and societie
> that I ought to have done.   My uncl told me that I was quarreld
> with by others for unkindnes, nor having so open a hart as my father.

James is busy with all the final arrangements, but he confesses " I miss a spiritual fram in goeing about this sorrowful
action."   There is only five years of the son's diary, which
breaks off in 1685.   He did not die till 1708 and it is probable that he kept a diary all his life, like his father.   James
Brodie was subjected to fines and punishments on account
of his alleged frequenting of Conventicles.   He married Lady
Mary Ker, daughter of the third Earl of Lothian, but he
never attained any prominent position.   In diary writing he
adopts his father's style and phraseology and even his spelling.   In the general tone of self-depreciation a page of the
one very much resembles a page of the other.   But one
misses the shrewd judicial reflections of the older man and
James is a little freer in style and more 'critical of other
people :

> visited Lord Forbes by the way.   I found him crabbed and ill to
> please.
>
>   I went to Forres to a meiting of the heritors . . . oh !   so ill as
> all ar filld. what corrupt, unsound men.

My nevey, James Dunbar, in him I sie much dissolutnes and deboshrie, want of education, want of nurtur : he has drunk in a great deal of evil.

He is often occupied in cutting timber, but he expresses no affection for trees or nature. James, in fact, seems to be a colourless reproduction of his father, although no doubt, if we had all his diary, we should be able to get a more complete picture of him.

WILLIAM CUNNINGHAM OF CRAIGENDS

A CCOUNTS when they are elaborately kept and carefully dated can be more illuminating than scrappy objective diary entries. From the Diary and Household Book of William Cunningham of Craigends, which he kept between 1673 and 1680, we can learn much of the domestic life and manners of the time.

For instance, the punctilious entry of his purchases of clothes gives us a complete outward picture of him. He must have been rather dressy. Even the mending of " ane old piriwick " is recorded, as is also the " soalling of stockins." For rough weather and riding he had " great bend-leather boots," " threed stirrup stockins " and " ryding tapped stockins." While playing at bowls he wore " a pair of coarse gloves." For dress occasions he had " silk stockins " fastened with " a pair of broidered garters," silver buckled shoes, coat and breeches of " purpur cloath " fixed with ties made from " fifteen ells of purpur ribbon." His breeches were strengthened at the knee with " searge " and his coat was lined with " calico " or " Black taffetee." One suit, though furnished with nine dozen silver buckles, required " a dozen more silver buttons " to complete the number of its metal fastenings. His " good gloves " were " shivrons " specially procured from " St. Johnstoun," the great seat of kid glove manufacture. His sleeves and cravat were of " camrick " bordered with lace. Over his dress he wore a belt in which his sword and scabbard held place ; on his head was his " piriwick " and over the periwig was set a " cawdebink " or French hat. On horseback he wore a " velvet Cap." For morning he had a " mourning cloke " with ten dozen buttons. At other times his cloak was of Baragon or Paragon, so called from the excellence of its material, manufactured in Italy.   He had also a " Jastycoat " or tightly fitting body coat with forty-two buttons, while the " westcoat " or under doublet had four dozen.   Cunningham was most careful of his " razours " which were sent to Glasgow " to be sharped " ; and for his hair he had not only bone but also two " timber " combs, " a little pocket brush " and a supply of " sweet hair powder."   Cunningham undoubtedly must have been a bit of a dandy.

He lived at Craigends with his wife, a daughter of Lord Ruthven, and his father and mother and sisters.   The joint household kept a common table, the young couple paying their parents for board in terms of agreements of which he gives full details.   This patriarchal household was governed by " the lady," his mother.   The terms of his engagement of servants are elaborately set down.   We may give one extract showing that Cunningham, like so many others, had trouble with his servants :

My boy Andrew Grey having run away I agreed with one Thomas Clerk, a tailour, to serve me for a man.   The Condition was 10 pounds of fie till Martimas being then 8 months to it (for he was presently to enter) Ane suit of old cloaths of my casting to serve him for wear for the whole year if he should stay ; and 2 or 3 pair of shoo's als I should cast them.   So Thomas Clerk entered but would not come West tho' it was his condition to come on his foot (wee travelling in coach) As also I gave him 24s to bear his charges besides 9s I gave him a feeing, and ane pair of old shoo's.   But he deceived me, and came not West and when I wrote for him David Lamsdaill sent me George Marshall in his place who would serve me upon the same condition, getting only 24s for his charges West, which I payed him out of 3lb my wife was owing me.

For the most part the entries are a record of business transactions.   They are, as he says, " all my civill adoes that are worth the marking," such as the following :

I closed with my mother about the half year's boarding from Whits till Mart[s]. 1675.   I gave her 256 Mks in money and counted the Achans 12 stane of cheese (which she got) at 24 mks, Inde 250 Mks.   This with 19 bowls of my meal and 6 bowls of my bear payed the sd half year's boarding, according to the old rate.

The black horse which I got from Archbald Arthur having fallen crooked in my hand, I sold him to John Shaw for five pound sterling which he could not promise to pay me before Whitsunday next.

Nevertheless, we can gather here and there from these business entries and from the accounts a good deal about the diarist. For instance, he makes " payment for prognostications," which shows he was superstitious. We find, too, that he played tennis, hunted, curled, played at bowls, billiards and cards. In Edinburgh he visits " the play," witnesses " rope dancing," sees " the bears and the ape " and has " a sight of the elephant." Cunningham's library does not appear to have been very extensive. Only small sums are expended on the purchase of books, which were all of a theological character. The frequent occurrence of gifts to beggars " at the gate " or " in the road " gives some idea of how the country was overrun with beggars at that time.

The diary and accounts were published by the Scottish History Society in 1887.

PATRICK, FIRST EARL OF STRATHMORE

"THE Book of Record," compiled by Patrick Earl of Strathmore has several elements in it which cannot be described as private diary writing. Nevertheless, the vellum-bound folio volume, with its elongated flap tied round to cover the front edges of the book, contains in its curious way the life-story of a great Scottish nobleman. There is a section devoted to autobiography, a large number of purely business entries and very elaborate and detailed accounts of his restoration and decoration of his castles of Glamis and Castle Lyon. Born in 1642, he succeeded to his estates in 1660 and restored the fortunes of his family. He was made a Privy Councillor in 1682 and was Lord of Sessions (1686–9). Although he had strong Jacobite leanings, he eventually took the oath to King William in 1690.

The first 110 folios are written from his dictation in the handwriting of Thomas Crombie, his confidential servant. In 1685 Crombie ceased to write and after an interval of three years Lord Strathmore himself takes up the pen and in a clear, bold, legible hand fills in the last nineteen folios. He begins at this point with an explanation of his motive :

'Here is a long surcease of what I am very unaccountable for ; for this three years I have neglected to wreat memorialls of my transactions. But I conceave it is a thing very necessar both for the ease of one's own memory, and ther present satisfaction, to the end when all is recorded posterity may see and be convinced of ther not being unprofitable in there generation, and may be induced by good example to follow the good and to eschew what may be amiss in the management. Tho. I take God to witness it has been and is the outmost indeavour of my life to order all my affairs both for the honour credit and preservation of my family.'

The servant who wrote the former part of this book went abroad w^t my second son, after wch Having six moneths at leave, and in some more disuse of pains and application from that tyme till now I was instant enow and at the head of my own affairs, but delayed making or continuing the record of what I did, trusting the same to my memory.   But that now finding myself at a loss therby, and being resolved to sett all down w^t my own hand and not to commit it to a serv^{ts} wreating, who may be here to day and away the morrow, I hope by being punctuall therin, and by what is writ'ne before and hereafter shall make up the loss of thes three years memor's for from the tyme I left and discontinued my wreating till now it is no less than full three years and some odd moneths.

Lord Strathmore was the son of John Earl of Kinghorne, who by bad management and extravagance had encumbered his estate with heavy debts.   Patrick succeeded by a long course of economy and self-denial not only to free the estate from the burden of debt, but to enhance its value and leave his two castles in splendid condition.   It is in the auto-biography that we learn most about him, and it would be tempting to quote from it.   His estimate of his own character may be given because it is just and he lived up to it :

By Divine providence, which I may rather ascrive it to then out of any choice of my owne, being then so young and of no experience, I did then begin, and still have continued, with just and equall dealings to all men.   I never defrauded the poor, nor had I ever any favour or ease from those who were powerfull, allwayes acknowledg-ing my father's bonds when I saw them.   And I hope, by the mercie of God, founding againe my familie upon the pillar of justice, I shall be able to transmitt a good pairt of my estate with much less of incumbrance and debt then I found att my entrie thereto.

The dated entries are almost exclusively of a business character, and largely concern the restoration of his castles. He admits :

I have saved many a pond and pennie but I acknowledge a great deal of weakness in my humour that way inclining to be verie profuse upon all things of ornament for my houses as I have been upon building.

Sample entries with regard to building may be given :

I agried with him in the month of feb^y 1688, and albeit I managed it w^t all the care and precaution possible (for some eight years agoe or more for doore and chimney peices at Castle lyon when the reforms of that house were compleeted, and divers picturs then done which are in the great hall of Glams or elsewher thorow the house he had then near about as much of my money) yet the painting of the roof of my hye dinning roume off the great Hall, The ovall of the cheif bed chamber and my chappall which stood him I'm sure more then half a years work, arose to a considerable summe of money.

I here include all the Chimney and doore peices of both storeys of the west syde of this hous of Glammiss, off the floor of both halls, all together stand me nynety pound sterline, and his bed and boord in the family, wch soume of nynety pound sterline is accordingly payed him and discharged upon the back of the Contract wch I have layed up in my cabinet at Ed^r.

The following entry shows he employed women house painters and also discloses his method with his workmen :

I have also agried with two English women hous painters, who have been a considerable tyme here, The acct whereof when ther work is finished shall be sett down. The most p^{rt} of ther tyme my family has been at Castle Lyon, but when it's here, they have also the benefit of ther meat in the house. And tho. I hold it as a rule to agree w^t workmen so as not to have the trouble of feeding them, for in some cases, if they know off no imploy^t elsewhere they prolong the work for the benefit of having ther meat bound to their mouth, yet such as thes painters and the more ingenious sort of craftsmen coming from places at a distance, ther is a necessity of being liberall that way.

And ev'ne of masons and wrights wher a man has much adoe, It is expedient to have a heads man over the rest, who must also have something of this nature done to them. Tho. ev'ne it's frequently losed that is done that way, for they are apt enow to receive the favour w^t out any rebatement of the pryce of ther work. And the only way not to be cheated is to have no work.

His payments to his workmen are generally partly in money and partly in meal. There was a custom in the seventeenth and eighteenth centuries by which workmen began work at 5 a.m., had an hour for breakfast, 8 till 9 : an hour and a half for dinner, 12 to 1.30, and a further half hour from 4 to 4.30, which was called the " four hours drink." Lord Strathmore seems to have objected to this latter custom when he writes in an " Observ^{ne} anent workmen " :

I chuse much rather to pay a very full and competent pryce to all kind of work men then to be in use of waisting meall and malt and allowing them morning drink and four-hours wch was the custom long ago : but that I have worn it out of use, finding too tho. it was much yet these kind of cattell being in use of it considered it very little.

He also enters his purchases :

Mr. Cockburn the Goldsmith bought a parcell of his plate to the value of a 1500 lib. sterl.   Of this plate I choiced out eleven dishes great and small such as fitted best the table I intend to serve w^t them, wch weigh about but upwards of eight hundred ounces.   The plate of intrinsick value if 3 lib. 4ss. p ounce, I agreed to acct. it and 6ss. p ounce, some of the dishes being splite new and the rest very little worse, he puts out the former graving and do's myne of new. This amounts to 3000 lib. scots. for wch I have giv'ne bond payable at Whits. next and he keeps the plate in his custody till pay^t be made. Ther is also a chaffing dish.
    I have also bought of Bailzie Brand in Edin^r a Cabinet for my fyne bed chamber, a very large looking glass for the drawing roume, Table and Hands of Italian paste, very fine, and other two speciall good glasses, I give for all four score pound sterline payable at Whits nixt.

There is a note of his arrangements for allowances for his wife and daughter :

Resolved upon this as an easier way rather then to obleidge my wyfe still to be att the trouble to apply to me upon everie litle occa-sione for money and so have ordered six hundered ponds scotts to be payed to her in four equall parts according to the four quarters of the yeare be my factors.   Merti. last was the first terme and Candle-mes last was the second wch is payed.
    Siclyke to teach my eldest daughter a little management and to know the species of money.   There is att the same termes and Divi-sions a hunder pond payed and to be payed to her whereof two termes are past and payed.

The book of Record leaves off abruptly on June 18, 1689. In this month Lord Strathmore was engaged in a conspiracy with the Earl of Southesk and others for the purpose of raising troops to create a diversion in the North of Scotland in favour of James II.   There is one entry towards the end which gives some hint of this :

I did outreike two horse in Angus and one in Perthshyre for the levy of horse and had difficulty enow in pleasing the officers, w^t ther ryders and arms.

It is curious that on his return, when he had become a reconciled supporter of King William, he did not fill more of the many blank pages in the great folio volume. He died in 1695.

The book of Record is carefully transcribed with notes and introduction by A. H. Millar in the Scottish History Society's volume for 1890.

GEORGE RIDPATH

ADVERSE criticism of editors of diaries has been in many cases unavoidable. It is a pleasure therefore to find an editor to whom unstinted praise may be accorded. Sir James Balfour Paul, who edits the Diary of George Ridpath in one of the volumes of the Scottish History Society, has got a true perception of the valuable elements in diary writing. He sees precisely how to reach a man and estimate his character through his diary entries. When he is obliged to make cuts from the voluminous manuscript before him, he may be trusted not to omit any of the illuminating sidelights which too often an editor dismisses as trivial and irrelevant. Ridpath, like many diarists, chronicles public events. These passages are omitted because, as the editor rightly says, such information can always be got in the ordinary history books. Sir James defends his method in a passage in his introduction, which may be quoted because it gives weighty support to the argument so often repeated in these volumes that the subjective rather than the objective side of diary writing and the intimate rather than the public references are the most significant in making a true analysis of a human document.

"If it is objected," says the editor, "that with these omissions we are left with a chronicle of very small beer, it may be replied that it is just this small beer that we need and that is so refreshing. Reports of big things in life are easily found, but it is less easy to get information as to the daily life of the people, their reading, their dinners and drinkings, their quarrels and reconciliations, their loves and hates, their little jaunts painfully accomplished for the most part over very inferior roads and, generally, the home life of the period."

George Ridpath, who came of a Border family, was born
in 1717 and educated at the University of Edinburgh. He
was licensed to the Presbytery of Chirnside in 1742 and two
years later he was presented to the parish of Stichel, where
he remained till his death in 1772. The two manuscript
volumes of his diary now extant cover the period from 1755
to 1761.

The diary contains no material of public importance and
on the private side there is nothing spicy or scandalous which
might attract the more frivolous reader. But it is a good
instance of a regular journal written without the slightest
idea of ultimate publication which reflects with faithfulness
the personality of the writer. Yet there is no introspection
and a refreshing absence of the spiritual rhapsodies and morbid
self-dissection which are so common in diaries of the period.
The personality disclosed is that of an unpretentious, broad-
minded and highly cultivated man. As we peruse his regular
daily entries we feel sure he must have been as a companion,
a friend, and later a husband, one of those people of rare
quality who in spite of their obscurity, as judged by the
orthodox historical standards, have possibly reached a higher
point in human and spiritual development than many whose
names are writ large on the pages of history. And we gather
this not from philosophic dissertations or political opinions
but from his daily pursuits and passing comments on men
and books.

We have an instance here, too, of a diary where the author
makes no attempt whatever to explain himself, analyse his
feelings or paint his own portrait, and yet by his very reticence
quite unintentionally discloses to us not by phrases or confessions but by the quiet regularity of his objective record a
true picture of himself.

Ridpath wrote about 170 years ago, but his style is aston-
ishingly modern. In spite of his great culture he shows no
trace of pedantry or of any self-conscious or sententious
effort when he relates the events of the day. But he has a
way of expressing himself at times which shows his distinction of mind and his sensitive intelligence. Ridpath was an
omnivorous reader and a keen gardener. There is hardly

an entry without mention of or comment on the book he is reading, and on most days he writes " wrought in the garden " and gives some account of his gardening operations, with notes on the weather.   As a reader he was no perfunctory skimmer of books but a close student and critic.   He read everything that came to hand, but hardly any fiction and practically no theology.   Solid volumes of the classics and history engage his daily attention.   He often notes the book he has at his bedside : " slept on Horace," " slept on Kennets *Roman Antiq.*," " slept on Plautus's *Amphitruo*, which is very droll."   We may quote some of his literary judgments and give some extracts showing how reading and gardening were combined :

Wrought much in the garden and some in the glebe. Read a little of Voltaire's third part. The former two parts are from a surreptitious copy and he seems to promise an improved edition of them. This part he owns and proposes to continue the Work till he connect it with his Louis XIV. He is always lively and entertaining.

Planted my tulips and ranunculuses tho' the ground is rather too wet yet ; did not care to delay it longer. . . . Read some of the beginning of the *Athenian History* in order to prepare for reading Stanley's *account of Solon*.

Richardson came here after breakfast and staid till after dinner. Read as yesterday and wrought a little in the garden. 'Tis an infinite pity, and what Millar deserves to be whipt for, that Stanley should be printed so incorrectly.

Read the rest of the account of Aristotle's Philosophy in Stanley. His account of the Morals is very paltry, being taken from Hobarus. What he extracts from the originals himself is far better done. Evening read some of Cicero's *Familiar Epistles*. Am now going to read them and the *Letters to Alficus* by Varns. Slept on Horace whom I have scarce opened since I read his Odes with Francis's Translation in the spring.

Read some in the fifth volume of Dodsley's *Miscellanies* and in the afternoon and evening about 100 pages of the first and second volume of *Parliamentary History*. What may be the value of this work as a compilation I know not but for the original part of it, at least of this parcel, it is, in the matter, poor and jejune, and, in language, groveling, mean and inaccurate. Strange that England should be doomed to such historians !

His broad-minded appreciation of *Candide* he shows in the following entry :

> Tho' it has much the appearance of being graceless and athiestical yet I am not sure if it contains much more than just satire on the presumption of Philosophers in pretending to explain or account for particular phenomena of Providence from their systems and partial views. The conclusion of the whole is excellent, *travailler sans raisonner, c'est le seul moyen de rendre la vie supportable.*

Ridpath complains sometimes of being too tired to read and this is not surprising when we note his great activities as a parish minister. He was no student recluse. But he was shy and found difficulty in getting on with strangers. There is just a passing gleam of self-revelation in the middle of a long passage he writes after a visit to Edinburgh :

> To live agreeably at Edinburgh, I find it would be necessary for me to live in a Lodging where I would be at perfect liberty ; to be well equipped in point of dress and to associate more with people of speculation and learning than those of gayer turn ; yet not altogether to avoid the latter. But the greatest disadvantage of all for that sort of life is my want of facility in making up to strangers and conversing with them. A disadvantage partly from complexion but chiefly from education, and my ordinary train of life that I believe I shall never wholly get over.

As a preacher he was not remarkable. His sermons were often very long ("far too long," "beyond all bounds "), and probably very dull. Although he always writes on Saturday, "prepared for to-morrow," and on Sunday gives the text of the sermon, nothing that he says shows that he is particularly interested in this part of his work. On the other hand, not only did he constantly visit the sick, but his interest in medicine makes him record in his diary the fullest medical details which in most cases the editor has omitted as being quite unprintable. He notes his own symptoms too.

Ridpath was not an ascetic. He liked a night out with his friends, is "soberly very joyous," but occasionally the mirth is "more wild than elegant." "We drank a good deal of punch after dinner and were very good company."

Quieter evenings are " spent very merrily " and the company
entertain themselves with cross-questions, chess, crambo,
rebuses and drawing profiles, and one evening he himself
" furnishes a new catch." But he does not like dissipation
or too much gossip ; " was rather disturbed than entertained
by their everlasting clack." Ridpath can be very critical
about people. Of one acquaintance he says, " Tis a pity
the man should be so idle and such a burr," of another " never
was such an idle dangler." The following is a severe description of a couple :

Patterson looks like fifty, is heavy and of a man behaviour, whence
it may be concluded that the animal who has clung to him and
followed him so far, is not of the highest order. We saw her next
morning. She is not un-handsome, seems to be very young and her
mein and behaviour show her to be quite raw and low bred.

And here is a disappointing beauty :

Saw the young Beauty who has a pretty face also a neat little
person. But her face scarce expresses anything but pertness, her
voice coarse, her manner of speaking rapid and disagreeable, and
her look or mein nothing of that sweetness or softness feminine which
is so ready to captivate so that it is a little odd she should have
married for love. But tastes are infinite.

He is, however, a great appreciator of feminine beauty :
" a fine girlie," he says of one, " and abundantly pretty."
Of another, whom he refers to as " the Naid," he remarks
that she

has lost something of the natural innocence and simplicity of her
manners which was one of her greatest charms. Yet she is still a
lovely lassie.

But it soon becomes clear which of the company he meets
is his favourite. Torn pages and erasures, however, prevent
us from hearing as much about her as we should like. Minna
Dawson is at first referred to casually, but we can see he
takes an interest in her when he says : " she is sore thinned."
The three or four lines describing his proposal are charming :

Minna Dawson called in her way from Sir Robert's to Newton. Attended her to the planting, and there, on the mossy turf under a sweet grove first told her in words my desire of making her my own. *Quod faustum felixque sit.*

A few days later he has " some explicatory chat with her about what passed on Tuesday." After this her name occurs often ; he takes her about " en croupe " when he rides (the equivalent of the modern carrier of a motor bicycle). " Walked down to Kelso with my dear lassie and carried her back again on horseback." His proposal was in July, 1760, but he did not marry Minna till September, 1764. He eventually had a son and two daughters, but as he died in 1772 his married life was short, but we feel convinced it was happy. Where Minna is concerned the entries are spoilt by erasures. When re-reading his diary Ridpath probably felt shy and cut out the passage where the rapture of love had run away with his pen.

He gives a full and pathetic narrative describing the death of his niece Nancy. We are given in great detail all the incidents of the sick-room and of his patient attendance till the end :

The sweet little innocent at last expired betwixt 7 and 8 in the morning of Wednesday the 14th at the age of 8 years. I performed all the duty to her I could, by sitting up all the night by her and from time to time administering to her some little draughts part of which she with great efforts got over, till within a few hours of her death. She knew me and looked on me often with pleasure ; attempted also to speak to me but could not articulate her words. Thus it pleased God to remove a great ornament and comfort to the parents and all our family in the beautiful blossom of tender, tho' seemingly very vigerous youth.

The Diary is a very pleasant record of an active, whole-some and intellectual life. It is regularly kept, and if he misses a day through illness or for any other reason he does not fill the gap with a summary of the interval. There is no attempt on his part to magnify his own importance and he certainly avoids the style which he condemns in another who, he says, was " prompted by vanity to babble to posterity what he dares not mutter to his contemporaries."

5

But in his exact description of the day's events he gives a very complete idea of the customs and habits of his times, and while there is nothing to excite the reader's attention in his doings we never lose our interest in the writer.

MARJORIE FLEMMING

WE have had instances of diaries begun at an early age by lifelong diarists in which the earlier entries are not specially notable. It seems probable that people have generally lost or destroyed their earlier efforts at diary writing and any genuine childish attempts to record thoughts and incidents are rare. But here we have a child's diary which is absolutely unique. Marjorie Flemming died when she was seven years old. Fortunately of her writings which have been preserved diary entries form a considerable portion. In her very brief span of life she managed to leave a reputation behind her which has no parallel. She is the one child authoress mentioned in the *Dictionary of National Biography*.

Marjorie Flemming, Pet Marjorie or "Maidie," as Sir Walter Scott used to call her, was born in 1803. She was the daughter of James Flemming, a magistrate of Kirkcaldy, but she lived with her aunt, Mrs. Keith, who was a friend of Scott's. Maidie was constantly with Scott, who would carry her off from her home in the folds of his shepherd's plaid and read to her and make her recite. " She's the most extraordinary creature I ever met with," he told Mrs. Keith, " and her repeating of Shakespeare overpowers me as nothing else does." She was writing excellent letters before she was six, and several of her poems exist. Humour and poetic fancy run through all she wrote and her diary in all probability was just one of the channels for her curiously precocious desire for expression.

One is very much tempted to quote passages from Marjorie's *magnum opus*, which was a poem on Mary Queen of Scots. Her admiration for her heroine is balanced by her

hatred of Queen Elizabeth.   Just a few lines must be allowed
to show Marjorie's style as a poetess :

> She flew to England for protection
> For Elizabeth was her connection
> Elizabeth was quite cross and sour
> She wished poor Mary in her power.

Fortunately in the diary entries we have enough to show
us a child mind with a very unusual gift of expression.   It
is the real child, not the infant prodigy, which appeals to
us.   No faked child diary, no effort of a grown-up to work
up their childish productions can bear the same stamp of
pure authenticity which the pages of Marjorie's journal
present.

The origin of the diary was an attempt of Isa Keith, her
cousin, to improve Marjorie's handwriting and spelling.   A
copybook was given to her in which she was to write down
whatever came into her head and in the original manuscript
Isa's corrections and comments appear.   The manuscript
books have disappeared, but fortunately Dr. John Brown,
to whom they were handed, had a complete copy made of
them.   From time to time when the spelling becomes very
bad or the handwriting careless Isa's comments are written
across the page, " Careless Marjorie," " Marjorie must write
no more journal till she writes better."   But we feel sure,
although a disciplinarian, Isa Keith knew well enough the
precious treasure these pages contained.

But the difficulty of selection is almost insuperable, as in
practically every entry there are passages worth quoting for
their perspicacity, humour, or curious originality.   All we
can do is to go through the Journals lifting selections as we
pass subject to the restraint of the space at our disposal.
At any rate no comments or explanations are necessary.
We must remember that Marjorie was just six years old
when the Journal begins.

The Divil is curced and all his works.   Tis a fine book Newton on
the profecies.

I wonder if another book of poems comes near the bible ; the
Divel always grins at the sight of the bibles ; bibles did I say ? nay

at the word virtue. I should like to learn Astronomy and Geography; Miss Potune is very fat she pretends to be very learned she says she saw a stone that dropt from the skies but she is a good christian. An annibabtist is a thing I am not a member of; I am a Pisplikan (Episcopalian) just now and a Prisbeteren at Kercaldy my native town which though dirty is clein in the country; sentiment is what I am not acquainted with though I wish it and should like to practise it I wish I had a great deal of gratitude in my heart and in all my body. The English have great power over the franch; Ah me peradventure at this moment some noble Colnel at this moment sinks to the ground without breath; and in convulsive pangs dies; it is a melancholy consideration.

Love I think is in the fasion for everybody is marring there is a new novel published named Self control a very good maxim forsooth.

In the love novels all the heroins are very desperate Isabella will not allow me to speak about lovers and heroins and tiss too refined for my taste. a lodestone is a curious thing indeed it is true Heroick love doth never win disgrace this is my maxim and I will follow it for ever.

Grandure reagns in London and in Edinburgh there are a great many balls and routs but none here. The childish distempers are very frequent just now. Tomson is a beautifull author and Pope but nothing is like Shakespear of which I have a little knolege of.

Love is a papithatick thing as well as troublesom and tiresome but O Isabella forbids me to speak about it.

Expostulations of all kinds are very frivolous. Isabella thinks this nonsense so I will say no more about Expostulations.

There is a book that is caled the Newgate Calendar that contains all the Murders; all the murders did I say, nay all Thefts and Forgeries that ever were committed and fills me with horror and consternation.

I am overpowered with the warmness of the day and the warmness of the fire and it is altogether unsufferable though there is a good deal of wind.

I pretended to write to a lord yesterday named Lord Roseberry about killing crows and rooks that inhabit his castle or estate but we should excuse My Lord for his foolishness for as people think I think Too for people think he is a little derangeed.

Isabella this morning taught me some Franch words one of which is bon suar the interpretation is good morning.

If any mans wife marry another when her husband is yet alive everybody will hate her and she shall be the object of there derision and there disgust. . . . Macarry is not yet transported it must be a dreadful thing transportation. God Almighty knows everything that we do or say and he can kill you in a moment. Bishop Sandford excels Mr. James in preaching Lying is the high road to theft and murder King John is a beautiful play and so is Richard 3. I never saw a play acted in my life. Anybody that does not do well are very miserable and unhappy and not contented.

This is the final entry in the first journal, which was written in Edinburgh. While writing the second journal she was chiefly at Braehead. It begins in a very dashing way :

The day of my existence here has been delightful and enchanting. On Saturday I expected no less than three well-made Bucks the names of whom is here advertized : Mr Geo Crakey and Wm Keith and Jn Keith the first is the funniest of everyone of them. Mr Crakey and I walked to Crakyhall hand in hand in Innocence and matitation sweet thinking on the kind love which flows in our tender-hearted mind which is overflowing with majestick pleasure. Nobody was ever so polite to me in the hole state of my existence. Mr Crakey you must know is a great Buck and pretty good looking.

I confess that I have been more like a little young Devil than a creature for when Isabella went up the stairs to teach me religion and my multiplication and to be good and all my other lessons I stamped with my feet and threw my new hat which she made on the ground and was sulky and was dreadfully passionate but she never whiped me. . . .

Yesterday I behave extremely ill in God's most holy Church for I would never attand myself nor let Isabella attand which was a great crime for she often tells me that when to or three are gathered together God is in the midst of them and it was the same Divel that tempted Job that tempted me I am sure but he resisted satan though he had boils and many many other misfortunes which I have escaped. I am now going to tell you about the horrible and wretched plaege that my multiplication gives me you cant conceive it—the most Devilish thing is 8 times 8 and 7 times 7. it is what nature itselfe cant endure.

Today I pronounced a word which should never come out of a ladys lips it was that I called John a Impudent Bitch and Isabella afterwards told me that I should never say it even in a joke but she kindly forgave me because I said that I would not do it again I will tell you what I think made me in so bad a humour is I got 1 or 2 cups of that bad bad sina tea to Day.

Isabella teaches me to or three hours every day in reading and writing and arethmatick and many other things religion into the bargan. On Sunday she teaches me to be virtuous.

This is Saturday and I am very glad of it because I have play half of the day and I get money too—but alas I owe Isabella 4 pence ; for I am finned 2 pence whenever I bite my nails. Isa is teaching me to make Simecolings nots of interrigations peorids and commas etc. As this is Sunday I will meditate uppon senciable and Religious subjects first I should be very thankful I am not a beggar as many are.

It is melancholy to think that I have so many talents and many there are that have not had the attention paid to them that I have and yet they contrive to be better than me.

Now am I quite happy for I am going tomorrow to a delightfull place Braehead by name belonging to Mr Craford where there is ducks cocks hens bubbyjocks 2 dogs 2 cats and swine ; which is delightful.

Every morn I awake before Isa and Oh I wish to be up and out with the larkies but I must take care of Isa who when aslipe is as beautiful as Viness and Jupiter in the skies ;

I am going to tell you of a melancholy story. A young Turkie of 2 or 3 month old would you believe it the father broak its leg and he killed another I think he should be transported or hanged.

I am going to tell you that in all my life I never behaved so ill for when Isa bid me go out of the room I would not go and when Isa came to the room I threw my book at her in a dreadful passion and she did not lick me but said go into room and pray and I did it.

I am going to turn over a new life and am going to be a very good girl and be obedient to Isa Keith here there is planty of goosberys which makes my teeth water.

My religion is greatly falling off because I dont pray with so much attention when I am saying my prayers and my character is lost among the Braehead people I hope I will be religious agoin but as for regaining my character I despare for it.

everybody just now hates me and I deserve it for I dont behave well.

This is Thursday and it was frosty but the sun shins in all its beauty it is very romantick indeed.

Isabella and Miss Isabella Craford walks to Baronbugal and jump with filisity over wals and fences.

The end of this journal is filled up with words written out

to practise her spelling. In 1810, when she was just seven,
she began her third journal.

Osian's poems are most beautiful I am very strong and robust
and not of the delicate sex.

Some days ago Isabella had a terrable fit of the toothake and she
walked with a long nightshift at dead of night like a gost and I
thought she was one. She prayed for tired natures sweet rest ever
balmy sleep but did not get it a ghostly figure she was indeed enought
to make a saint tremble it made me quever and shike from top to
toe but I soon got the better of it and next morning I quite forgot
it Superstition is a very mean thing and should be dispised and
shuned.

I am reading the misteries of adolpho with Isabella and am much
interested with them. I have got some of Popes works by hart and
like them very much.

An address to my father when he came to Edinburgh.
My father from Kircaldy came but not to plunder or to game.
Gameing he shuns I am very sure   He has a heart that is very pure
Honest and well behaved is he
And busy as a little Bee.
I am very fond of some parts of Tomsons seasons
I like loud Mirement and laughter.

I love to walk in lonely solitude and leave the bustel of the nosey
town behind me and while I look on nothing but what strikes the
eye with sights of bliss and then I think myself trinsported far beyond
the reach of the wicked sons of men where there is nothing but strife
and envying pifering and murder where neither contentment nor
retirement dwells but there dwells drunkeness.

I should like to go and see the curosities in London but I should
be affraid of the robbers For that country is greatly infested with
them at Edinburgh their is not so many of them.

In this journal she frequently breaks into poetry. One
example may be given :

I love in Isa's bed to lie
O such a joy and luxury
The bottom of the bed I sleep
and with great care I myself keep
Oft I embrace her feet of lillys
But she has got on all the pillies
Her neck I never can embrace
But I do hug her feet in place

But I am sure I am contented
And of my follies am repented
I am sure I'd rather be
In a small bed at liberty.

Underneath this there is written upside down as a footnote :

At Braehead I lay at the foot of the bed becase Isabella says I disturbed her repose at night by continial figiting and kicking but I was very continialy at work reading the Arabin nights entertainments which I could not have done had I slept at the top. I am reading the Mysteries of adolpho and am much interested in the fate of poor poor Emily.

The last page in the last journal is signed and dated " Marjory Fleming Kirkaldy July 19." She had left the Keiths and returned to her parents at Kirkcaldy. She continued to correspond with her beloved Isa, but not for long. In December of the same year, 1811, she fell ill with measles and just as it seemed as if she were going to recover she died.

The Diary and her poems and letters are set out in full in *The Story of Pet Marjorie*, by L. Macbean, and picturesque descriptions of Walter Scott's association with her are given in Dr. John Brown's *Horæ Subsecivæ*.

SIR WALTER SCOTT

THERE would probably be a general consensus of opinion that Sir Walter Scott's diary can be ranked among the half-dozen best, although there might be differences of opinion as to some of the other five. It would, however, be difficult to say what other diary it resembles. Diaries are good for very different reasons. There is nothing of Pepys' intimate gossip in Sir Walter Scott's style ; he does not record conversations and describe at length scenes like Fanny Burney, he does not collect gems from the Great like Crabb Robinson ; he has nothing of the violence and passion of Haydon ; nor does he rake out the inner recesses of his mind like Barbellion. He writes what is in his thoughts with a delightful intimate frankness, and the supreme merit of the diary he left, lies in the fact that he wrote it because he liked writing it so much, not because, like many other diarists, he thought he ought to write it. The diary, therefore, becomes an excellent medium for his transparent honesty. It never occurred to him to write a diary till 1825, when he was fifty-four ; so we have only the record of seven years. That he was dependent on making it into a very regular habit is shown by what he writes after a break of a few months :

Having omitted to carry on my Diary for two or three days, I lost heart to make it up and left it unfilled for many a month and day. . . . I half grieve to take up my pen and doubt if it is worth while to record such an infinite quantity of nothing, but hang it ! I hate to be beat, so here goes for better behaviour.

He regrets not having kept a diary in earlier years and Byron's attempt attracts him. But he is far more regular and methodical in his habits than Byron ever was and although there are lapses, he may be counted as a regular

74

daily writer. In the first months he delights in it, "I am enamoured of my journal," "I think this journal will suit me well," and addresses it as "O revered Jurnal!"; and then he has a doubt that it gives a wrong impression of himself. "By the way, how intolerably selfish this Journal makes me seem—so much attention to one's naturals and non-naturals!" He reads Johnson's very bad advice to Boswell when he kept a diary, "to omit registers of the weather and like trumpery" and he says : "I am resolved in future not to register what is yet more futile—my gleams of bright and clouded temper." Fortunately he could not keep this resolution if he went on writing at all, not that Scott was ever morbid or introspective. But he has an engagingly restrained way of reflecting his mood, and omits repetitions which bore him. "It is well enough to ride every day but confoundedly tiresome to write it down." He was not addicted to psychological analysis, but there is sometimes shrewd penetration into motive and mood which prevents the diary being merely a record of events. But in describing events and even handling anecdotes appropriately his literary skill makes this chronicle of his life the most delightful reading. There is no self-conscious attempt at self-portraiture, and therefore the portrait we get is lifelike. All this makes the task of detaching passages extremely difficult. The best way will be to make extracts of his reflections on his health, his record of his work, his moods and tastes, and his comments on people and incidents.

Scott did not like making too many notes about his health, but as a real diarist he is occasionally forced to. "My Journal is getting a vile chirurgical aspect," he says after suffering from a chill, and again, "I shall tire of my Journal if it is to contain nothing but biles, plasters and unguents." But at moments there is a note of real depression :

There is some new subject of complaint every moment ; your sicknesses come thicker and thicker ; your comforting and sympathising friends fewer and fewer ; for why should they sorrow for the course of nature ? The recollection of youth and uninterrupted powers of activity neither improved nor enjoyed is a poor strain of comfort. The best is, the long halt will arrive at last and cure all.

Towards the end, when more serious illnesses occur, he is obliged to notice them :

I was frightened by a species of fit which I had in February, which took from me my power of speaking.   I am told it is from the stomach. It looked woundy like palsy or apoplexy.   Well, be it what it will, I can stand it.

I walk with great pain in the whole limb and am at every minute during an hour's walk reminded of my mortality.   I should not care for all this if I was sure of dying handsomely. . . .   But the fear is the blow be not sufficient to destroy life and that I should linger on an idiot and a show.

No more need be said about health because on the whole it figures remarkably little in the diary.   About his work he writes a great deal—not only arrangements about publication and precise facts about the amount of work done, but interesting thoughts about method and inclination.   In the majority of entries some reference to his work occurs, sometimes only a few words, " writing very heavily," " I was not very cleever today," " I wrote hard today," " scribbled away lustily," " I am become a sort of writing automaton " ; but often he says much more :

I wrote six of my close pages yesterday which is about twenty four pages in print.   What is more I think it comes oft twangingly. The story is so very interesting in itself and there is no fear of the book (Life of Napoleon) answering.   Superficial it must be but I do not disown the charge.   Better a superficial book which brings well and strikingly together the known and acknowledged facts, than a dull boring narrative, pausing to see further into a millstone at every moment than the nature of a millstone admits.   Nothing is so tiresome as walking through some beautiful scene with a minute philosopher, a botanist, or pebble gatherer, who is eternally calling your attention from the grand features of the natural scenery to look at grasses and chucky stones.

It is odd, when I set myself to work *Doggedly,* as Dr. Johnson would say, I am exactly the same man that I ever was, neither low spirited nor *distrait.*   In prosperous times I have sometimes felt my fancy and powers of language flag, but adversity is to me at least a tonic and bracer ; the fountain is awakened from its inmost recesses, as if the spirit of affliction had troubled it in its passage.

The half hour between waking and rising has all my life proved propitious to any task which was exercising my invention.   When I get over any knotty difficulty in a story or have had in former times to fill up a passage in a poem, it was always when I first opened my eyes that the desired ideas thronged upon me. This is so much the case that I am in the habit of relying upon it, and saying to myself when I am at a loss " Never mind, we shall have it at seven o'clock tomorrow morning."

Having ended the second volume of *Woodstock* last night, I have to begin the third this morning. Now I have not the slightest idea how the story is to be wound up to a catastrophe. I am just in the same case as I used to be when I lost myself in former days in some country to which I was a stranger. I always pushed for the pleasantest road and either found or made it the nearest. It is the same in writing, I never could lay down a plan—or having laid it down, I never could adhere to it.

Wrote to the end of the chapter and knowing no more than the man in the moon what comes next.

There is one thing I believe peculiar to me—I work, that is, meditate for the purpose of working, best, when I have a *quasi* engagement with some other book for example. When I find myself doing ill or like to come to a standstill in writing I take up some slight book, a novel or the like and usually have not read far ere my difficulties are removed and I am ready to write again. There must be two currents of ideas going on in my mind at the same time or perhaps the slighter occupation serves like a woman's wheel or stocking to ballast the mind, as it were, by preventing the thoughts from wandering and so give the deeper current the power to flow undisturbed. I always laugh when I hear people say, Do one thing at once. I have done a dozen things at once all my life.

Scott was wrong in thinking the phenomenon he described in the above entry was peculiar to him. This habit shows how little he adopted the concentrated and confined outlook of the specialist.

Let us take one day of confessed idleness :

A most delicious day in the course of which I have not done
" The least right thing."
Before breakfast I employed myself in airing my old bibliomaniacal hobby, entering all the books lately acquired into a temporary catalogue, so as to have them shelved or marked. After breakfast I went out, the day being delightful—warm yet cooled with a gentle breeze, all around delicious ; the rich luxuriant green refreshing the eye, soft to the tread and perfume to the smell. Wandered about and looked at my plantations. Came home and received a visit

from Sir Adam.   Loitered in the library till dinner time.   If there
is anything to be done at all today it must be in the evening.   But
I fear there will be nothing.   One can't work always *nowther*.
Neque semper arcum tendit Apollo.
There's warrant for it.

And here is a description of his day a year or so before he
died :

Rise at quarter before seven ; at quarter after nine breakfast
with eggs or in the singular number at least ; before breakfast private
letters etc. after breakfast Mr. Laidlaw comes at ten and we write
together till one.   I am greatly helped by this excellent man, who
takes pains to write a good hand, and supplies the want of my own
fingers as far as another person can.   We work seriously at the
task of the day till one o'clock when I sometimes walk—not often
however having failed in strength and suffering great pain even from
a very short walk.   Oftener I take the pony for an hour or two and
ride about the doors ; the exercise is humbling enough, for I require
to be lifted on horseback by two servants and one goes with me to
take care I do not fall off and break my bones, a catastrophe very like
to happen.   My proud promenade à pied or à cheval, as it happens,
concludes by three o'clock.   An hour intervenes for making up my
journal or such light work.   At four comes dinner—a plate of broth
or soup, much condemned by the doctors, a bit of plain meat, no
liquors stronger than small beer, and so I sit quiet till six o'clock,
where Mr Laidlaw returns and remains with me till nine or three
quarters past, as it happens.   Then I have a bowl of porridge and
milk which I eat with the appetite of a child.   I forgot to say that
after dinner I am allowed half a glass of whiskey or gin made into
weak grog.   I never wish for any more nor do I in my secret soul
long for cigars, though once so fond of them.   About six hours a
day is good working if I can keep at it.

There is an entry in 1827 which shows how amusing he
can be about trifles and how through trifles he is led on to
reach deep into the philosophy of life :

The contrast of leaving Abbotsford to former departures is of an
agitating and violent description.   Assorting papers and so forth.
I never could help admiring the concatenation between Ahitophel's
setting his house in order and hanging himself.   The one seems to
me to follow the other as a matter of course.   I don't mind the
trouble though my head swims with it.   I do not mind meeting
accounts, which unpaid remind you of your distress, or paid serve
to show you you have been throwing away money you would be
glad to have back again.   I do not mind the strange contradictory

mode of papers hiding themselves that you wish to see and others thrusting themselves into your hand to confuse and bewilder you. There is a clergyman's letter about the Scottish pronunciation to which I had written an answer some weeks since (the parson is an ass, by the bye). But I had laid aside my answer being unable to find the letter which bore his address ; and in the course of this day, both his letter with the address and my answer which wanted the address, fell into my hands half a dozen times, but separately always. This was the positive malice of some hobgoblin and I submit it as such. But what frightens and disgusts me is those fearful letters from those who have been long dead, to those who linger on their way fare through this valley of tears. These fine lines of Spenser came into my head. " When midnight o'er the pathless skies." Ay, and can I forget the author !—the frightful moral of his own vision. What is this world ? A dream within a dream—as we grow older each step is an awakening. The youth awakes as he thinks from childhood—the full grown man despises the pursuits of youth as visionary—the old man looks on manhood as a feverish dream. The Grave the last sleep ?—no : it is the last and final awakening.

The beauty of the entries in Scott's diary is that he is just having a chat with himself and nearly always enjoying it. In fact he writes as a motto on the first page of the first volume :

> " As I walked by myself
> I talked to myself
> and thus myself said to me."

Passage after passage shows without any effort his predilections and foibles, his preferences and his prejudices, and above all, his enjoyment of life.

He is bored with flashy company :

Talking of Abbotsford it begins to be haunted by too much company of every kind, but especially foreigners. I do not like them. I hate fine waistcoats and breast pins upon dirty shirts.

But he does not like solitude :

I like the hermit life indifferent well, nor would, I sometimes think, break my heart, were I to be in that magic mountain where food was regularly supplied by ministering genii and plenty of books were accessible without the least intervention of human society. But this is thinking like a fool. Solitude is only agreeable when the power of having society is removed to a short space and can be commanded at pleasure. " It is not good for a man to be alone."

It blunts our faculties and freezes our active virtues. And now, my watch pointing to Noon, I think after four hours work I may indulge myself with a walk. The dogs see me about to shut my desk and intimate their happiness by caresses and whining. By your leave, Messrs Genii of the Mountain library, if I come to your retreat I'll bring my dogs with me.

He appreciates solitary moments for " castle building —this wielding of the aerial trowel—" and confesses, " since I was five years old I cannot remember the time when I had not some ideal part to play for my own solitary amuse-ment." This childlike buoyancy is very attractive and the passages in which his naturally happy disposition insists on asserting itself are among the best of all :

Did I ever pass unhappy years anywhere ?   None that I remember save those at the High School which I thoroughly detested on account of the confinement.   I disliked serving in my father's office, too, from the same hatred of restraint.   In other respects I have had unhappy days—unhappy weeks—even on one or two occasions unhappy months ; but Fortunes finger has never been able to play a dirge on me for a quarter of a year together.

Here are parts of two consecutive entries on leaving Edin-burgh and returning to Abbotsford in 1826 :

July 13.   Today I leave Mrs Brown's lodgings. Altogether I cannot complain but the insects were voracious even until last night when the turtle soup and champagne ought to have made me sleep like a top.   But I have done a monstrous sight of work here notwith-standing the indolence of this last week which must and shall be amended.

> So good-by Mrs Brown,
> I am going out of town,
> Over dale, over down,
> Where bugs bite not,
> Where lodgers fight not,
> Where below you chairmen drink not,
> Where beside you gutters stink not ;
> But all is fresh and clean and gay
> And merry lambkins sports and play,
> And they toss with rakes uncommonly short hay,
> Which looks as if it had been sown only the other day,
> And where oats are at twenty five shillings a boll, they say,
> But all's one for that, since I must and will away.

July 14. Abbotsford. Arrived here yesterday before five o'clock. Anybody would think, from the fal-de-ral conclusion of my journal yesterday that I left town in a very gay humour—*cujus contrarium verum est.* But nature has given me a kind of buoyancy, I know not what to call it, that mingles even with my deepest afflictions and most gloomy hours. I have a secret pride—I fancy it will be so most truly termed—which impels me to mix with my distresses strange snatches of mirth " which have no mirth in them."

He refused to allow the slings and arrows to upset him and cultivated an unconcern as to what was going to be the next shaft of fortune. " A feather just lighted on the ground can scarce be less concerned where the next blast may carry it."

When confined by " this bitch of rheumatism," he writes :

I regret God's free air as much as any man but I could amuse myself were it in the Bastille.

Something of the black dog still hanging about me ; but I will shake him 'off. I generally affect good spirits in company of my family whether I am enjoying them or not. It is too severe to sadden the harmless mirth of others by suffering your own causeless melancholy to be seen ; and this species of exertion is, like virtue, its own reward ; for the good spirits, which are at first simulated, become at length real.

But he knows well what depression means :

Real affliction has something in it by which it is sanctified. It is a weight which, however oppressive, may like a bar of iron be conveniently disposed on the sufferer's person. But the insubstantiality of a hypochondriac affection is one of its greatest torments. You have a huge feather bed on your shoulders which rather encumbers and oppresses you than calls forth strength and exertion to bear it. There is something like madness in that opinion and yet it has a touch of reality.

Scott genuinely hated having a fuss made over him :

As a literary man I cannot affect to despise public applause ; as a private gentleman I have always been embarrassed and displeased with popular clamours, even when in my favour. I know very well the breath of which such shouts are composed, and am sensible those who applaud me today would be as ready to toss me tomorrow ; and I would not have them think that I put such value on their favour as would make me for an instant fear their displeasure. Now all this declamation is sincere, and yet it sounds affected.

But he goes on to say that he would not hide himself to avoid applause which "probably no one will think of conferring," and he tells an amusing anecdote of a woman in Carlisle in 1745 who in great fear shut herself up in a closet in order to escape ravishment by the Scottish soldiers. As time passed no one disturbed her solitude till at last in her impatience she popped her head out of the door and asked, "Good folks, can you tell me when the ravishing is going to begin?"

A grateful admirer sends him an embarrassing present:

Here is a whimsical subject of affliction. Mr. Harper, a settler, who went from this country to Botany Bay, thinking himself obliged to me for a recommendation to General M'Allister and Sir Thomas Brisbane has thought proper to bring me home a couple of Emus. I wish his gratitude had either taken a different turn or remained as quiescent as that of others'whom I have obliged more materially. I at first accepted the creatures, conceiving them, in my ignorance to be some sort of blue and green parrot, which, though I do not admire their noise, might scream and yell at their pleasure if hung up in the hall among the armour. But your emu it seems stands six feet high on his stocking soles and is little better than a kind of cassowary or ostrich. Hang them! they might eat up my collection of old arms for what I know. It reminds me of the story of the adjutant birds in Theodore Hook's novel. No; I'll no Emuses!

When in Paris, where he is of course lionized, he writes:

A great number of ladies of the first rank were present and if honeyed words from pretty lips could surfeit I had enough of them. One can swallow a great deal of whipped cream, to be sure, and it does not hurt an old stomach.

Although the shower of compliments makes him wish for "a little of the old Scotch causticity," he amuses himself at dinners and parties. Of his knowledge of the language he says:

As to French, I speak it as it comes, and like Doeg in Absalom and Achitophel

"— dash on through thick and thin
Through sense and nonsense, never out nor in."

Some may be surprised at Scott writing "I don't much love children." But he makes an exception of the child he is mentioning, " a fine merry little girl," and, as we know, another notable exception was Pet Marjorie. Indeed, this means that he was a true lover of children because he discriminated. People who say they " love children " might just as well say that they " like houses."

Although a poet, Scott was no musician. He confesses, " I am like Jeremy in *Love for Love*—have a reasonable good ear for a jig but your solos and sonatas give me the spleen."

The Diary during the period Scott was in London is much less good. Of course he sees a number of interesting people. But he finds it as difficult as any diarist does to make interesting people with well-known names appear interesting when he writes about them. Moreover, he seems to have had little superficial discrimination in judging strangers of note. His description of George IV is almost absurdly fulsome. He " converses with ease and elegance " ; he is " the model of a British monarch " ; he is " every inch a King " and so forth. There might have been a good deal more to say about the Duchess of Kent than that she was " very pleasing and affable." And of the Duke of Wellington one would expect something more than a note of " the frank manners of this unequalled pride of British war," who received him " with all his usual kindness." It is the same with Madame D'Arblay and many others. Indeed one might believe that celebrities were unusually dull people if one took the estimate of them from diaries, even from the diaries of other celebrities. Haydon seems to be the only diarist who could hit them off in a sentence or too. Sir Walter knew Haydon, but not of course as a diarist. He contributed to a fund to help the unfortunate man and afterwards sat for his portrait. Of Haydon he says : " He is certainly a clever fellow, but somewhat too enthusiastic, which distress he seems to have cured in some degree." This again is very inadequate.

When, however, Scott knows his subject well, his analysis of character is interesting. Archibald Constable of course he knew intimately. His unfortunate financial straits were directly or indirectly connected with the house of Constable & Co. When he dies Scott sums him up :

Constable was a violent tempered man with those he dared use freedom with. He was easily overawed with people of consequence, but, as usual, took it out of those whom poverty made subservient to him. Yet he was generous and far from bad hearted. In person goodlooking but very corpulent latterly ; a large feeder and deep drinker, till his health became weak. He died of water on the chest, which the natural strength of his constitution set long at defiance. I have no reason to regret him ; yet I do. If he deceived me, he also deceived himself.

The money troubles which were his constant worry recur frequently through his diary. It will be remembered that the collapse of Messrs. Constable involved the failure of Scott's printing firm, Messrs. Ballantyne & Co., and the last years of his life were consequently devoted to the attempt of clearing off by his pen the huge debt for which he found himself responsible. He wanted, if he could, to save Abbotsford :

Yet to save Abbotsford I would attempt all that was possible. My heart clings to the place I have created. There is scarce a tree on it that does not owe its being to me and the pain of leaving it is greater than I can tell.

This is part of a very long entry in which he expresses his doubts and fears and writes several times during the day—a good example of how he was treating his diary as his confidant, because as he says :

I *am* pleased to be left to my own regrets without being melted by condolences, though of the most sincere and affectionate kind.

But Scott's nature would not allow the burden which fell on him to produce a melancholy which might emerge in most of his entries. On the other hand, the courage with which he faced the catastrophe is very apparent :

I feel neither dishonoured nor broken down by the bad—now really bad news I have received. I have walked my last on the domains I have planted—sate the last time in the halls I have built. But death would have taken them from me if misfortune had spared them. My poor people whom I loved so well ! There is just another die to turn up against me in this run of ill-luck ; i.e. if I should break my magic wand in the fall from this elephant, and lose my popularity with my fortune. . . . But I find my eyes moistening and that will not do. I will not yield without a fight for it. . . . Poor Mr Pole the harper sent to offer me £500 or £600 probably his all. There is much good in the world after all. But I will involve no friend, either rich or poor. My own right hand shall do it—else will I be *done* in the slang language and *undone* in common parlance.

He refers later to a batch of bills which he finds on his return home :

Greeted by a few small accounts whistling like grape shot.

Just as he curbed self-pity, so did he object to the insincerity which too often accompanies woe. This passage on funerals must be given although it is long :

I hate funerals—always did. There is such a mixture of mummery with real grief—the actual mourners perhaps heart-broken, and all the rest making solemn faces and whispering observations on the weather and public news and here and there a greedy fellow enjoying the cake and wine. To me it is a farce full of most tragical mirth, and I am not sorry but glad that I shall not see my own. This is a most unfilial tendency of mine, for my father absolutely loved a funeral ; and as he was a man of fine presence and looked the mourner well, he was asked to every interment of distinction. He seemed to preserve the list of a whole bead-roll of cousins merely from the pleasure of being at their funerals. . . . I saw the poor childs funeral from a distance. Ah that Distance ! What a magician for conjuring up scenes of joy or sorrow, smoothing all asperities, reconciling all incongruities, veiling all absurdness, softening every coarseness, doubling every effect by the influence of the imagination. . . . Even so the distant funeral the few mourners on horseback, with their plaids wrapped around them—the father heading the procession as they enter the river, and pointing out the ford by which his darling is to be carried on the last long road—not one of the subordinate figures in discord with the general tone of the incident—seeming just accessories, and no more—this *is* affecting.

Of his wife's death he writes very simply and without exaggeration, and he refers afterwards in a sentence or two from time to time to his consciousness of the loss of her companionship. He liked to have people about him who caused him no effort. There is a vivid touch of domestic homeliness in such a sentence which occurs at the end of an entry as : " My wife and girl's tongues are chatting in a lively manner in the drawing-room. It does me good to hear them."

The entry when Lady Scott dies is a long one. We may reverently take one or two extracts from it :

I am as alert at thinking and deciding as ever I was in my life. Yet when I contrast what this place now is, with what it has been not long since, I think my heart will break.   Lonely, aged, deprived of my family—all but poor Anne, an impoverished embarrassed man, I am deprived of the sharer of my thoughts and counsels who could always talk down my sense of the calamitous apprehensions which break the heart that must bear them alone.   Even her foibles were of service to me, by giving me things to think of beyond my weary self-reflections. . . .   I wonder how I shall do with the large portion of thoughts which were hers for thirty years.   I suspect they will be hers yet for a long time at least.   But I will not blaze cambric and crape in the public eye like a disconsolate widower, the most affected of all characters.

Towards the end when he is abroad the diary becomes much more irregular and even Sir Walter Scott cannot make foreign travel interesting.   In fact this great diary illustrates perfectly in itself the general truth with regard to all diaries. When the water is still or rippled by the little cross-currents of pain and pleasure, the diarist is at his best ; he may be able to deal with a wave of adversity or misfortune, but when the breakers of great events, great people or great scenes come, a diarist is submerged and his efforts are futile.

Lovers of Scott's novels may be fewer than in days gone by, but time can only have increased the number of the lovers of his Journal.

JANE CAMERON
(MRS. MAWSON)

A N example of a diary of mental discipline kept by a woman may be found in the diary of Jane Cameron, written more or less regularly from 1829 to 1842. She had no idea of publication when writing, but after the birth of her daughter she seems to have wanted to save the book for her child's edification. Her object in writing is clear when she says :

> The perusal of the past mercies of God which I have written down has often created in me stronger desires after holiness ; it has at times proved a cordial to me when ready to faint by the way, for I have been reminded that He who blest me in times past is still the same Immutable God.

Her illnesses and the weather are the only other subjects mentioned beyond her religious experiences. Her style is conventional, stilted and long-winded, and as in so many other diaries of this description actual incidents are covered over with commonplace moralizing. She never travels beyond a few miles from her home, her music is hymns, her painting the illumination of texts. Her activities do not range beyond collecting for missions, teaching in Sunday school, and holding Temperance meetings. Her anticipations of the future are invariably gloomy. If she passes a pleasant evening with friends she feels sure some disaster is at hand ; whenever an anniversary comes round she wonders whether she will survive to see another and during every trifling ailment she prepares to meet her God. The gloating over death, in which she and all her circle indulged, is shown by the following entry recording a visit to some friends whose son William had been drowned while bathing:

When walking in the garden Mr. A observed to Miss A " William, my dear, planted this bush ; let us take care of it " said he as he drew a circle round it with his cane. What a conflict of feeling was there ! It was truly affecting. Some boxwood in another part of the garden attracted our attention as being very high, it wanted cutting " It might " Miss A said " but my deceased sister planted it and we touch it not." Thus in that lovely spot mortality was continually remembered.

When her brother dies she suffers such mental anguish that a disbelief in the very existence of God seizes her. She finally records, however, that " The Lord enabled me to triumph in His great might."

She rejects suitors on the grounds of their insufficient religion, but while she is convinced that anything agreeable to her feelings must be wrong, she finally succumbs and marries an ambitious young tradesman of Newcastle. Worldly cares form a large part of her married life, and having other openings for her emotions and activities her religion loses its rather hysterical violence. She and her husband become Unitarians.

She has no talent for describing character, but there are several entries in the diary about her little girl :

1840. L's birthday. Her character. She is twelve months old today and in excellent health. We already perceive the unfolding of the mind. She gives evidence of a quick, positive lively disposition. She is particularly imitative and strikingly fond of company evincing great delight in the presence of strangers and manifests great dislike to be withdrawn from them. She seldom cries ; but has lately got into frequent fits of irritation. This evil we are truly solicitous to check and therefore avoid crossing her needlessly.

This sounds as if Jane was an indulgent mother, but she says later that she made it a rule never to give the child what she cried for, and by the time she was two the little girl was being chastised for her faults and had in other respects a serious upbringing :

Last week when at tea I noticed my little dear unceremoniously taking a few grains of sugar out of the basin. I told her she ought not to do so. She immediately replied with a most serious countenance ' God see me ' I took up her words and talked to her on the subject. Who can question a child's capability of instruction, when one at the tender age of two and a half could give so prompt and correct a reply.

The child lost her mother when she was four years old.

The only public event mentioned in the diary is the outbreak of cholera in 1832, which Jane calls the plague. The diary is typical more than individual. Extracts from it were published in a small memoir privately printed in 1846 in Newcastle, where she lived ; but the editor cut out most of the mundane matter in his anxiety to preserve intact the religious meditations.

Miss Hope Dodds, a granddaughter of Mr. Mawson, has kindly furnished full particulars with regard to the diary, the original manuscript of which is in the possession of the diarist's daughter.

ANNE CHALMERS

I am very partial to English clergymen. They are very agreeable though generally of short stature. They have such amiable smiles.

NOTHING could be more promising than this as a diary entry. Unfortunately Anne Chalmers only kept a diary for one year at the age of seventeen when she was visiting England in 1830 with her father, Dr. Thomas Chalmers, the famous Scottish Divine and Professor. In that year, however, she made daily entries, giving full details of all that occurred with the punctilious exactitude of a child and the shrewd powers of observation of a much older person. We get a fuller description of a visit to the Zoo than of incidents which were perhaps of graver importance. But her enjoyment of and excitement over the life she was living make every entry of Anne's eminently readable.

Directly she embarks on her journey she sits down and describes her fellow-passengers on " the celebrated steamship the *United Kingdom* " :

Miss Steward was (I suppose) a young lady and evidently meant to be a fine lady. She and her friend Miss Anstruther kept most of the people in the ladies' cabin awake for three hours one night while they discussed sandwiches and talked nonsense, wondering whether the people were asleep, for they were very quiet, as if it were possible to sleep while they talked so loud.

Her first impression of London is not very favourable :

Our lodgings in London are in a narrow street and are dirty, sooty and uncomfortable. The paper of the sitting room has glaring yellow roses on a red ground and the bedrooms are musty and airless. They say to make things better that it is a very fashionable street but what is fashion ? I can't tell but you may " ask of Folly for she her worth can best express." I sat moping and exclaiming against London all the rest of the evening.

Not only the ordinary clergy but Bishops especially arrest her attention :

I begin to like bishops very much. I regard them with the eye of a naturalist as a new species before unknown to me. Deans wear aprons and single-breasted coats, the same as bishops, but they have not the strangely shaped wigs nor the three-cornered hats which distinguish the latter. There were very nice bishops to-night. Winchester was at Sir T. Acland's the other night, also Lichfield and Coventry. I saw a young bishop at St James's one day, but Bath and Wells who was at the Anti-Slavery meeting is the ugliest person of the species I have seen. Winchester is ten years younger and handsomer than his brother Chester and is a richer and superior bishop and wears a badge ; but Chester is very agreeable and they are both good men. The Bishop of London is very handsome.

She is in a great state of excitement at meeting Brougham. She writes his name in capitals, keeps her eye on him all through a service at the Temple Church and describes him as " very animated." She attends debates in both Houses of Parliament. In the House of Lords her *penchant* for bishops reappears when she says, " The bench of bishops looks more elegant than any other part of the House." In the House of Commons she is critical :

Immediately after dinner we went to the House of Commons, found Mr Hay waiting for us, who conducted us to the ventilator where ladies can hear the speakers and even see them sometimes through the holes in the roof. We found a good many ladies there, among others two very gay ones who laughed in convulsions at some of the members who came under this scrutiny. ' Oh ! Good God ! What a pair of eyes ! I declare he is looking up ! La ! What frights in boots ! I could speak better myself ! ' and various similar instructive and amusing exclamations formed the tenor of the conversation. But to return to the business of the House. Its members do not sit gravely and sedately on their benches as wise legislators ought to do. . . . They walk about and talk to each other unless an interesting person is speaking and call out ' Hear ! hear ! Order ! ' —I suppose at random for they certainly do not *seem* to pay much attention. Then they like so much to exercise their privilege of wearing their hats and appear constantly in boots, so that their general appearance is by no means dignified. . . . I did not admire the speaking very much but none of the eloquent men were there.

After a brief account of the debate, she writes at the end of the entry :

Really, Tuesday is a very eventful day for me, for the Tuesday before was the day on which I first stood on English ground and the Tuesday before that the first time I ever stood in a bucket on my way to the bottom of a coal pit.

At a dinner party Anne inadvertently experiences the sensations of intoxication which she describes :

I had only drunk a little wine and a very little champagne and taken a draught of beer, as I thought, but I am sure now it was strong ale. I felt as if my head was chaos itself, and something appeared to be rushing with immense force and rapidity through it but still I continued mechanically the usual operations of dinner though a sense of shame and horror overpowered me lest I should do anything extraordinary. I could hardly see anything but I was quite aware of my state and went regularly through my duties and answered the questions that were put to me with a calmness which I felt to be a horrible contrast to my real feelings. Happily it all subsided before dinner was over and my advice to every Scotchman is to beware of asking beer in London, for they invariably get either ale or porter.

She conceives a great admiration for a Mr. Forster, whom she describes as " the greatest man in Britain or perhaps in the world," and a Mr. Hall " who is about as great a man as Mr. Forster." The fame of these gentlemen unfortunately has not reached us to-day. They were, however, Dissenters, and Anne's admiration for the clergy of the Established Church makes her critical on this account.

I never saw anything like these Dissenters ; they would pull down Church and State and like the monkey in the Zoological Garden snatch the very wig from the Bishops' heads. I never got so completely into their set before, and it is really vexatious to see such men as Hall and Forster among them. I heard that two English clergymen called in the evening, and I wish I had seen them ; it would really have been refreshing.

She resents the compliments paid her by a Mr. Bennett and delicately suggests the reason for them :

he informed me that I was a lovely girl and always had been and would always continue to be so. I heard a whisper of his having partaken freely of the juice of the grape, and am inclined to believe

that, notwithstanding his sanctity, his want of tact allowed him to
overstep the quantity prudence would have assigned.

Among other celebrities she meets Samuel Wilberforce :

> He did so much work writing so many letters a day from a dozen
> to eighteen and preaching almost daily.   His neck, too, was so short.

She gives good descriptions of Anti-Slavery meetings, and
in addition to London life visits to other parts of England
are carefully described.   Her devotion to her father is very
apparent, and when she grew up her talent as a linguist
made her of considerable service to him.   In 1836 Anne
Chalmers married Dr. William Hanna.   In her old age Mrs.
Hanna wrote some retrospective autobiographical notes.   It
is a pity that her eminently successful attempt in 1830 did
not encourage her to become a lifelong diarist.   The notes,
her journal and her letters were collected together with some
biographical notices and published by her daughter in 1923.[1]

---

[1] Quotations from *Letters and Journals of Anne Chalmers* are given
with the kind consent of The Chelsea Publishing Co.

LORD COCKBURN

HENRY COCKBURN was a celebrated Scottish lawyer, judge and writer on legal matters. He compiled " memorials " of his times and continued this in a journal of public events between 1831 and 1854 which makes a valuable contemporary record of the development of the strife which issued in the disruption of the Scottish Kirk. The entry in 1843 in which he describes the event beginning " the crash is over " occupies no less than twenty-five printed pages. The whole journal is obviously written for publication and deals with political and legal events interspersed here and there with anecdotes. Cockburn had the reputation of being a genial and unconventional man and his style is by no means dull. But he hardly touches on personal and domestic affairs, or if he does it is quite formal, as for instance :

Mrs Cockburn being unwell was advised to sit in the open air a good deal.

In fact, he gives his views on writing of a private character in the following entry :

I have all my life had a bad habit of preserving letters and of keeping them all arranged and docqueted ; but seeing the future use that is often made of papers especially by *friendly* biographers who rarely hesitate to sacrifice confidence and delicacy to the promotion of sale or excitement, I have long resolved to send them all up the chimney in the form of smoke ; and yesterday the sentence was executed.

Travel occupies part of the journal and his weather reports are rather unusual. It is not the rainy day or the high wind which is noted at the moment when the writer is struck by it, nor is it the detailed meteorological record kept by some diarists. There is an occasional summary of the weather of a past period which a moment's reflection would have told him could be of no sort of interest to an eventual reader.

His comments on people are pointed and lively. Of Cobbett he says:

in 1793 he would have been sent to Botany Bay.

Of Macaulay:

he suffers severely from the vice of over talking and consequently of under listening.

Of Scott when he dies in 1838:

Dear Scott! When he was among us we thought we worshipped him at least as much as his modesty would permit. And now that he is gone we feel as if we had not enjoyed or cherished him half enough. How would we cling to him were he to reappear! It is a pleasure which the next generation may envy that I still hear his voice and see his form. I see him in the court and on the street, in company and by the Tweed. The plain dress, the guttural burred voice, the lame walk, the thoughtful heavy face with its mantling smile, the honest hearty manner, the joyous laugh, the sing song feeling recitation, the graphic story—they are all before me a hundred times a day.

We almost expect a personal impression when he takes his seat on the bench and becomes a lord. He begins:

This changes my whole life. I must cast off the old man and all his works.

But the considerations he proceeds to discuss are all of a purely professional character.

He often expresses enlightened and advanced views for his times, such as:

Popular education which is now the great fermenting subject is involved in no material difficulty in itself. Its difficulties arise almost entirely from religious repulsions. It is clear to my mind that keeping the popular education any longer in the hands of the Church is nonsense.

The regular diary writer, even if he be writing for publication, never can know when he is writing his last entry. There is seldom anything specially dramatic except in the bare

appearance of abruptness in a diary's end. In the case of
Cockburn he wrote five days before he died in 1854, when
he was seventy-five, a charming appreciation of a scene of
natural peace and beauty in the bay of Ayr, contrasting it
with the stuffy court where he had been presiding when on
circuit.

The two volumes were published in 1874.

JANE WELSH CARLYLE

THE revelations discovered in diaries may merely be, when they are read after many years, of historical value. Sometimes immediate descendants and friends who have known the diarist may be surprised by personal disclosures which they never suspected. But rarely can the diary of one who has died reveal to a contemporary some vital fact which in life was successfully concealed, and it would seem almost too dramatic if the contemporary happened to be the husband of the diarist. The shock he must receive becomes far greater owing to the source of the revelation being a private diary than if the information were derived from hearsay or letters. Yet this is what happened to Carlyle who first learnt from his wife's diary after her death how miserable she had been and learnt also that he himself had been in part the cause.

Jane Welsh Carlyle's diary kept between October, 1855, and June, 1856, is only a small fragment and it is noteworthy not only because of the disclosure it made to Carlyle but because of its intrinsic merit as a diary. It is not our business here to enter into the much discussed question of the relations between Carlyle and his wife, although certain facts must be referred to in order to explain some of the diary entries ; nor need we take into account Mrs. Carlyle's talents as a letter writer, because powers of literary expression, as many examples show, are not necessarily of any assistance at all in diary writing. But judging by the few entries which are available it would be no exaggeration to say that had Jane Welsh Carlyle's diary been available *in extenso*, it would have been one of the most remarkable diaries penned by man or woman. Even in this brief fragment we find glints of self-revelation ; we find ill-health and depression briefly referred to with moving reality and a quite exceptional power of graphic and humorous narration.

For instance, what could be duller and more utterly uninteresting than a visit to the dirty office of a Tax Commissioner to appeal against an income-tax assessment ? Yet this is how she relates it.

She makes up her mind to go because " If Mr. C. should go himself he would run his head against some post in his impatience, and besides for me, when it is over it will be over, whereas he would not get the better of it for twelve months—if ever at all."

Next day, after " not one wink of sleep the whole night through," she writes :

It was with feeling like the ghost of a dead dog, that I rose and dressed and drank my coffee, and then started for Kensington.   Mr C said ' the voice of honour seemed to call on him to go himself.'   But either it did not call loud enough or he would not listen to that charmer. I went in a cab to save my breath for appealing.   Set down at 30 Hornton Street, I found a dirty private-like house, only with Tax Office painted on the door.   A dirty woman-servant opened the door and told me the Commissioners would not be there for half an hour, but I might walk up.   There were already some half score of men assembled in the waiting room, among whom I saw the man who cleans our clocks and a young apothecary of Cheyne Walk. . . . Feeling in a false position I stood by myself at a window and ' thought shame ' (as children say).   Men trooped in till the small room was pretty well filled ; at last a woman showed herself.   O my ! did I ever know the value of any sort of woman—as woman—before ! By this time some benches had been brought in and I was sitting nearest the door.   The woman sat down on the same bench with me, and, misery acquainting one with strange bedfellows, we entered into conversation without having been introduced and I had ' the happiness,' as Allen termed it, ' of seeing a woman more miserable than myself.'   Two more women arrived at intervals, one a young girl of Dundee, ' sent by my uncle that's ill ' ; who looked to be always recapitulating inwardly what she had been told to say to the Commissioners. . . .   ' First-come lady ' called the Clerk opening a small side door and I stepped forward into a *grand peut-être* . . . a dim room where three men sat round a large table spread with papers.   One held a pen ready over an open ledger ; another was taking snuff and had taken worse in his time, to judge by his shaky, dazed appearance.   The third who was plainly the cock of the dung-heap, was sitting for Rhadamanthus—a Rhadamanthus without the

JANE WELSH CARLYLE

99

justice. ' Name ' said the horned-owl-looking individual holding
the pen. ' Carlyle.' ' What ? ' ' Car-lyle.' Seeing he looked
dubious I spelt it for him. ' Ha ! ' cried Rhadamanthus, a big,
bloodless-faced, insolent-looking fellow. ' What is this ? why is Mr
Carlyle not come himself ? Didn't he get a letter ordering him to
appear ? (She explains he received no such letter.) ' Huffgh !
Huffgh ! what does Mr Carlyle mean by saying he has no income
from his writings when he had himself fixed it in the beginning at a
hundred and fifty ? ' ' It means Sir, that in ceasing to write, one
ceases to be paid for writing and Mr Carlyle has published nothing
for several years.' ' Huffgh ! Huffgh ! I understand nothing
about that.' ' I do,' whispered the snufftaking Commissioner at my
ear. ' I can quite understand a literary man does not always make
money. I would take it off, for my share, but (sinking his voice
still lower) I am only one voice here, and not the most important.'
' There ' said I, handing to Rhadamanthus Chapman and Hall's
account ; ' that will prove Mr Carlyle's statement.' ' What am I to
make of that ? Huffgh ! We should have Mr Carlyle here to swear
to this before we believe it . . . we can make nothing of this ' flinging
my document contemptuously on the table. The horned owl picked
it up glanced over it while Rhadamanthus was tossing papers about,
and grumbling about people that wouldn't conform to rules.

Finally Rhadamanthus tells the horned owl to take off a
hundred pounds.

We must refrain from another quotation of an amusing
incident in a baker's shop, as the special interest of the diary
lies in other entries. But before giving extracts it is necessary to explain that Mrs. Carlyle greatly resented Carlyle's
infatuation at this time for Lady Ashburton. However much
her imagination may have magnified the circumstances the
fact remained that he was continually going to Bath House,
she felt the estrangement from him and consequently she
became intensely miserable. Here are some of the references
to her wretched depression :

I was cut short in my introduction last night by Mr C's return
from Bath House. That eternal Bath House I wonder how many
thousand miles Mr C has walked between there and here, putting it
all together ; setting up always another milestone and another betwixt
himself and me. Oh, good gracious ! when I first noticed that heavy
yellow house without knowing or caring to know, who it belonged
to, how far I was from dreaming that through years and years I
should carry every stone's weight of it on my heart.

Life gets to look for me like a sort of Kaleidoscope—a few things of different colours—black predominating—which fate shakes into new and ever new combinations, but always the same things over again.

My heart is very sore tonight, but I have promised not to make this journal a ' miserere ' so I will take a dose of morphia and do the impossible to sleep.

Alone this evening.   Lady A in town again ; and Mr C of course at Bath House.

> When I think of what I is
> And what I used to was
> I gin to think I've sold myself
> For very little cas.

Mended Mr C's dressing gown.   (A few days before she is mending Mr C's trousers.)   Much movement under the free sky is needful for me to keep my heart from throbbing up into my head and maddening it.   They must be comfortable people who have leisure to think about going to Heaven !   My constant and pressing anxiety is to keep out of Bedlam !   that's all . . . Ach !

Dear, dear !   What a sick day this has been with me.   Oh my mother !   Nobody sees when I am suffering now ; and I have learnt to suffer ' all to myself.'

It is not always that unjust treatment, harshness and disdain in her husband drives a woman *jusqu au désordre*, but it drives her to something, and something not to his advantage, any more than to **hers.**

I feel weaklier every day and my soul also is sore vexed—Oh how long !   I put myself in an omnibus, being unable to walk, and was carried to Islington and back again.   What a good shilling's-worth of exercise !

She is greatly troubled by her sleeplessness :

I hardly ever begin to write here that I am not tempted to break out into Jobisms about my bad nights.   How I keep on my legs and in my senses with such little snatches of sleep is a wonder to myself.

Here is a typical entry with a mention of Mazzini :

At last a fair morning to rise to, thanks God !   Mazzini never says ' thank God ' by any chance, but always ' thanks God ' ; and I find it sounds more grateful.   Fine weather outside in fact but indoors blowing the devil of a gale.

She never failed to see the humorous side of domestic
worries :

Oh good gracious alive ; what a whirlwind—or rather whirlpool—
of a day ! Breakfast had ' passed off ' better or worse and I was
at work on a picture-frame, my own invention, and pretending to
be a little work of art, when Mr C's bell rang like mad, and was
followed by cries of ' Come, come ! are you coming ? ' Arrived at
the second landing, three steps at a time, I saw Mr C and Ann in
the spare bedroom hazily through a waterfall ! The great cistern
had overflowed, and was raining and pouring down through the
new ceiling, and plashing upon the new carpet. All the baths and
basins in the house were quickly assembled on the floor, and I, on
my knees, mopping up with towels and sponges etc. In spite of this
disaster, and the shocking bad temper induced by it, I have to put
on my company face tonight and receive.

Two quotations may be given with some excellent comments on diary writing. She begins her first entry on October
21, 1855, by saying :

I remember Charles Buller saying of the Duchess de Praslin's
murder, ' What could a poor fellow do with a wife who kept a journal
but murder her ? ' There was a certain truth hidden in this light
remark. Your journal all about feelings aggravates whatever is
factitious and morbid in you ; that I have made experience of.
And now the only sort of journal I would keep should have to do
with what Mr Carlyle calls ' the fact of things.' It is very bleak
and barren, this fact of things, as I now see it—very ; and what
good is to result from writing of it in a paper book is more than I
can tell. But I have taken a notion to, and perhaps I shall blacken
more paper this time, when I begin quite promiscuously without
any moral end in view ; but just as the Scotch professor drank
whiskey, because I like it and because it is cheap.

After an interval of about three months, during which she
had neglected her diary, she writes in the following March :

We are now at the 24th of March 1856, and from this point of
time, my journal, let us renew our daily intercourse without looking
back. Looking back was not intended by nature, evidently, from
the fact that our eyes are in our faces and not in our hind heads.
Look straight before you, then, Jane Carlyle, and, if possible, not
over the heads of things either, into the distant vague. Look, above
all, at the duty nearest at hand, and what's more, do it. Ah the
spirit is willing, but the flesh is weak and four weeks of illness have
made mine weak as water.

In conclusion we may give Carlyle's own comment on the diary which shows there was a good deal more of it which was destroyed. " In 1856 too evidently, to whatever owing, my poor little darling was extremely miserable ! Of that year there is a bit of private diary by chance left unburnt, found by me since her death, and not to be destroyed, however tragical and sternly sad are parts of it. She had written, I sometimes knew (though she would never show to me or mortal any word of them), at different times, various bits of diary ; and was even at one time on a kind of autobiography (had not C——, the poor C—— now just gone, stept into it with swine's foot, most intrusively, though without ill intention,—finding it unlocked one day ;—and produced thereby an instantaneous burning of it ; and of all like it which existed at that time). Certain enough, she wrote various bits of diary and private record, unknown to me ; but never anything so sore, downhearted, harshly distressed and sad as certain pages (right sure am I !) which alone remain as specimen ! The rest are all burnt ; no trace of them, seek where I may."

SAMUEL CAMERON

A CONSCIENTIOUS desire for self-correction may be found in many diaries. Sometimes it takes the form of greatly exaggerated self-condemnation and sometimes of more moderately expressed resolutions for reform. The latter method characterizes the diary of the Rev. Samuel Cameron, who began writing at the age of twenty-four and continued the practice until within a day or two of his death in 1872. After taking his degree at Glasgow University he was appointed to his first charge in the Church of Scotland, which was a far-stretching strip of coast on the Mull of Kintyre. He was afterwards appointed to a very wide parish in the Highlands of Perthshire, where he remained till he died, refusing promotion which would have brought him more into the centre of things.

Although it has no specially remarkable features in it, the early diary reveals a man of some erudition, a scholar and a reader, and gives glimpses of the life of the crofters and fisher-folk among whom his lot was at first cast. A private journal of this kind kept partly for purposes of self-discipline and partly as time passes from habit, without the suspicion of a thought of publication, is always strongly coloured with the personality of the writer. Cameron is disclosed as an earnest and energetic worker with decided opinions and a high moral standard. He notes his sermons, which are often delivered in Gaelic, and he records his pursuits and the incidents of his life always with some personal comment. A curious feature is his use of Greek characters for names and sentences which are not any more private than other parts of his diary. For instance, he puts " the Queen's Coronation " in Greek characters and he actually writes out his accounts in the same way ; " a pair of trousers " written in Greek characters

103

is certainly peculiar. Latin quotations are frequently introduced and a few entries are written in Latin.

At the end of the year religious diarists often indulge in an
orgy of lamentation over their shortcomings. The following is refreshingly simple :

> Still labouring here in Saddell and Skipners—succeeding pretty
> well—at least I hear nothing to the contrary. I know myself some-
> what better, that is all I can say as to any change that may have
> taken place during the year that has now gone never to return.

A sermon :

> Preached among the rocks, the sea and myself trying which should
> roar loudest. It was not in one of its angry moods only chafed a
> little—so I carried the palm.

Here is a reference to the fishermen :

> The herring fleet have set their nets opposite us to-night, it is
> gloomy and blowy. Poor men they live a hardy life—they do not
> know much about the ease indulgence and luxury of the world ; it
> would be well if they knew as little of sin—not that they are remark-
> able in any way for immorality—but they are men and therefore
> tainted as every man is with that plague of the soul.

More extracts would show him critical but not censorious,
interested in public affairs and devoted to his work. But a
special mention may be made of a passage which shows that
his journal was the spokesman of his conscience. It is in
early years and he proceeds to have a long dialogue with
his conscience on the subject of early rising.

> (Says the conscience) " It is very foolish to spend the morning in
> bed it is the very best time for study."
> (To which he replies) " I know all that, say no more about it just
> now."

But his conscience is not to be put off and proceeds to
argue at length for a couple of pages.
Then he says :

> " True, true,—you have a very accurate memory for unpleasant
> recollections—have you none at all that are agreeable ? "
> " If I have not remember it is not my fault. I am but a journal—
> I tell nothing but what you committed to me—but I can summon up
> a few pleasing recollections also."

" Yes a few rarities *in gurgite vasto*."

" Will you get up in the morning, then perhaps I may henceforth add to these floating rarities."

And the conscience continues to argue and tell him he does not try.   The dialogue ends thus :

" Good-night little conscie."

" Good-night little as I am it is good for you that you have me otherwise . . ."

He notes the books he reads and occasionally he comments on public events.   There are several volumes of the diary. The original manuscript is in the possession of Miss Amy H. Cameron, of Edinburgh, the diarist's daughter, by whose kind permission the early part of the diary has been examined and the extracts made.

IRISH DIARIES

LIST OF IRISH DIARIES

ARRANGED IN CHRONOLOGICAL ORDER

Name of Diarist.	Occupation.	Date of Diary.	Source.	Page.
Richard Boyle .	1st Earl of Cork	1611–1642	*The Lismore Papers,* Vols. 1–5 (First Series), ed. by Rev. Alexander Grosart.	111
Mary Rich . .	Countess of Warwick	1666–1677	*Diary of Mary Rich,* Brit. Mus. MS. 27351–55 and 27358.	116
Elizabeth Freke	Wife of Percy Freke of Co. Cork	1671–1714	*Mrs. Elizabeth Freke her diary,* ed. by Mary Carbery, 1913. Cork Archæological Society, XVI.	120
Rowland Davies	Dean of Cork.	1689–1690	Camden Society, 1857.	127
John Scott . .	Divinity Student	1704–1708	*Two Centuries of Life in Down,* by J. Stevenson, 1920.	132
Jonathan Swift.	Dean of St. Patrick's ; man of letters	1710–1713	*The Journal to Stella.*	137
Lady Arabella Denny	—	1751	Original manuscript in the possession of Miss Amy Percival.	148
Wolfe Tone . .	Rebel . . .	1763–1798	*The Autobiography of Theobald Wolfe Tone,* ed. by R. Barry O'Brien, 1912.	153
John Fitzgerald.	Schoolmaster .	1793	Cork Historical and Archæological Society, Vols. 24–26.	162
Daniel O'Connell	Politician . .	1795–1802	*Daniel O'Connell : Early Life and Journal,* ed. by Arthur Houston, 1906.	166

Name of Diarist.	Occupation.	Date of Diary.	Source.	Page.
John Wilson Croker	Member of Parliament and man of letters	between 1810–1850	*Memoirs, Diaries and Correspondence of the Right Hon. John W. Croker*, ed. by Louis J. Jennings, 3 vols., 1884.	170
Tom Moore . .	Poet . . .	1818–1847	*Memoirs, Journal and Correspondence of Thomas Moore*, ed. by Lord John Russell, 8 vols. (1855). *Tom Moore's Diary*, ed. by J. B. Priestly, 1925.	174
John Mitchel .	Journalist and Agitator	1848–1853	*Jail Journal*, by John Mitchel, 1914.	184

RICHARD BOYLE,
1ST EARL OF CORK,
AND HIS DAUGHTER
MARY RICH, COUNTESS OF WARWICK

RICHARD BOYLE, the Irish statesman known as "the great Earl," went over to Ireland in 1588, and after early struggles, during which he saw more than once the inside of a prison, became escheator to the escheator general.   He purchased Sir Walter Raleigh's Irish possessions, out of which he rapidly acquired a large fortune.   He was knighted in 1603, given a peerage in 1616, and created Earl of Cork in 1620.   He was made Lord High Treasurer in 1631.   He worked persistently to undermine Strafford's authority in Ireland, and was probably largely responsible for his impeachment.   He died in 1643.

Much more, of course, might be related of his career, but this will suffice to show that he was an outstanding figure in the history of Ireland—rich, powerful, unscrupulous and autocratic.   From 1611 to 1642 he kept a diary and " remembrancer," which fills five quarto volumes of the *Lismore Papers*, beginning with a preliminary note on his ancestry. The diary consists largely of business entries, brief references to public events, his movements, legal matters, accounts of improvements to his house at Youghal, births and deaths, names of visitors and his loans and gifts.   A reader feels at once conscious of being in contact with a rich potentate of forceful character, high and mighty, dictatorial, lavish and grand with a good idea of his own importance, power and authority.   When he speaks in a controversy of holding " a sharpe and Lardge discourse " we feel that no one could

stand up to him.   There is a vein of superstition in the way
he always mentions the sign of the Zodiac when recording a
birth, and there is a certain humility in his references to the
Deity, but it is the humility of a great courtier not of a miserable sinner.   There is something rich even in his spelling.
His brother is " Bicsshop of Cork."   He " bestowed " on
him " a fayer young bay ambling gelding."   Geldings appear
very frequently among his presents.   When the " Bicsshop "
dies, he enters a solemn note, but wastes no time in trying
to get the position for another of his relations :

upon the firste notice thereof I posted my letters to the Lo. Deputy
to commend my cozen Richard Boyle Dean of Waterford to those
bicsshopricks.

When he goes over to England he has " long and graceous
Conference with the King's Majesty " and again " gracious
and private conference . . . in his bedd chamber at Royston
concerning Ireland and the government thereof."
He has profitable iron works, builds bridges, constructs
harbours and founds towns.
We find him actually raising and paying for troops which
he places under the command of his sons :

This daie the god of heaven bless, guide and protect them my three
sons, the Lord Dongarvan Kynalmeakie and Broghill, with the troop
of one hundreth horse that I supplied my son dongarvan with moneis
to raise, buy and arme, to serve his Ma^ty withall against his rebillows
Scottish subjects departed from me at Stalbridge ; god I beseech
him return them safe, happy and victoriows, to my comfort.

The following entries give us the atmosphere of jewels and
silk :

Delivered Mr. Ross to be made into a jewell for my wife XXX
small diamonds and XXVIII small Rubies which we.e set in a feather
of gold And at that tyme I delivered him XXXII orient pearles to be
holed and VI Irish pearls which she wears in a nycklease.

Paid for my blew bedd and my turcky table vi^ll and for my guylt
and green bedstedden with t..e fframes of the chair and 2 stooles
iiii^ll and for 5 yards of damask to make up the chair and stooles
1^s and to the uphoulster for sylck ffringe and making up the chaires
and stooles O and the windo cusshen of damask iii^ll.

His wife's petticoat is so valuable that it is worth handing on to one of his rich daughters :

I gave my wives best ritch petticoat which coste xxxv^{li} to my daughter digby and another I formerly gave my daughter Kate Jones and to my daughter countess of Barrymore my wives best inlayd cabbynett and to my daughter of Kildare the Ring full of diamonds that I paid a C marcks for to my L. Baltinglass

Even the tutor has to be suitably dressed :

I gave Mounsieur ffrances de Carey, my children's ffrench tutor, a veary good black silck grograme cloke lyned through with black ritch taffata and a black silk opograyn sute laced with embroidered satten laced and lyned with taffata.

He has his own " musicons " and there are several references to harps, one of which he lends to " Wm. Barry the blynd harper."

A harp also appears in a list of gifts each of which is accompanied by a small bottle of whisky, even in the case of the Archbishop of Canterbury :

My cozen Wm. Ryan sent me a faier new yrish Harp, which I sent to the Lo Keeper of England by Mr. pessly or rather by Edd. Hunt who carried him my lettres and to his Lady a Ronlet of vskebagh ; to my Lo. Archbishop of canterbury my lettres, with a watreford black firze to make him a cassock and a Ronlett of vskebagh.

Some more instances of his gifts may be quoted :

I gave my daughter, the countess of Barrymore a fair standing guilt cupp with a cover. And to my Ladie deyton a silver suger boxe of the skallop fashion for their New Years guyftes.

I presented my cozen, the Lady Smith with 2 suger loaves for her new years guifte, and with my great chedder cheese which the Lady Stafforde gave me in england ; and the Lady Smith sent me sixe cambrick handkerchers laced.

I gave Sir Charles Vavasor a bottle of Rosemary water which Thomas Williams mother gave me and two barrels of oates for his horses.

He lends money to Sir Walter Raleigh and many others and his gifts of geldings and other things are innumerable. Sometimes he receives a present :

8

My sister-in-law the Lady Brown bestowed on me a veary fair wrought purse of her own makinge.

Sir John dracott sent me a fresh sturgeon and the Maior of Waterford one hundreth of Lymons.

There are several notes about his servants :

one of my Skullery men called—did moste unfortunately by jesting with his knife run my undercook into the belly whereof he instantly died in my house in dublin.

When my coachman, Henry Allen, had served me above 9 yeares and was soe full of Aches and infirmities as he acknowledged he was unable to drive my coach noe longer he preferred Nichas Eloworth vnto me and there due to Harry 4^{11} I gave him 20 nobles and to him 30^s to paie his postillions.

He visits Eton and tips the boys very much like the modern parent, and he sends his own sons there :

1628   I came from Maidenhead to Eaton Colledg where I took my Lady Villiers her 3 sons and Mr. glanviles two sons to dynner with me to Windsore when I gave the 5 children xxx^s and that night, god be ever thancked, I and myne retorned all in safety to London.

1635   This day (the great god of heaven bless, guyde and protect them) I sent my two youngest sons ffrances and Robert Boyle with Carew their servant, under the chardge of my servant Thomas Badnedge from Lismoor to Yoghall to embarcque for England to be shooled and bredd at Eaton as my worthie frend Sir Henry Wotten, provost of Eaton collegd, should direct and order them, to whom I wrott to that purpose.

When he is made an earl he describes the event in magnificent language and ends :

Ffor this gread addicon of earthly honours God make me and my heires thanckfull to the Almighty and to his sacrd Ma^{ty} And that it maie continew unspotted in the name of the Boyles and my posteritie untill the end of the world—Amen.

The size of his family was in keeping with the rest of his opulence. He had fifteen children. Four of his sons were ennobled and seven of his daughters married noblemen. Deaths and births are all recorded.

Death of his wife in 1629 :

It pleased my mercifull god, for my manifold syns, this daye being the XVI of ffebrary 1629 between three and ffour in thafternoon of the same day, to translate out of this mortall world, to his glorious kingdome of heaven, the sowle of my deerest, deer wife who departed this world (to my unspeakable greef) at the Lorde Calfeylds howse in dublin ; ffor which heavy visittacon, god make me, and all myne, patiently thanckfull as becometh religeous christians, seeing it was none, but my own all knowing god that did it.

An illness :

This night my daughter Dongarvan fell sick and the next day being the last of this moneth the small pockes brake owt upon her.

Birth of a grandchild :

This daye being satterday and the seaventeenth day of Auguste 1639 abowt one o'clock in the afternoon, the sign being in Leo, or in the Hart and back, my daughter Katheryn Jones, was, god be ever praised, safely delivered at Stalbridge of her thirde child being a dawghter who for that it was borne about 40 daies before the mother's Reckoning was presently Xtned by the name of ffrances ; the Ladie Stafford and one Mrs Argent being the god mothers and Mr. danyell spicer, chapleyn the godfather ; god ever bless her.

There is a good account of how " my son Broghill " was secretly called away to fight a duel. The adversaries both returned without any wound, only Broghill took away " the ffrindg of Mr. Howard's glove with a passadg of his Rapier." It ended amicably, and they came home and supped together. The diarist concludes the entry " and all this for Mrs. Harrison." Mary, his seventh daughter and thirteenth child, is the one who causes him some trouble as we learn by the following entry :

The Lord Viscount Clandebieus son and heir Mr. James Hamylton with Mr. Treall his goomer and other his attendants came to Stalbridge and brought me lettres from his ffather. And being refuzed in Marriadge by my unruly daughter Mary he departed my hows the second of September to Bathe.

Further, he " deteigned " her allowance from her " not giving her one penny since the tyme for her disobedience in not marrying Mr. James Hamylton." He banished her to a little country seat near Hampton Court where Charles Rich visited her and married her in 1641.   The great Earl relented, paid her allowance and gave her a rich " marriadge porcon."

This Lady, who afterwards became Countess of Warwick, not only inherited her father's character, standing up to him and eventually making him give in, but also inherited his diary habit.   Her mother was Catherine, daughter of Sir Geoffrey Fenton, a scholar and statesman, who was Queen Elizabeth's secretary in Ireland and surveyor-general.

MARY RICH, COUNTESS OF WARWICK, became famous for her piety and charitable works.   She made her home at Leighs Priory, Felsted, referred to in her diary as " delicious Leez " and with other affectionate epithets.   She endeared herself to the family of her brother-in-law, Robert, the third Earl, while he was still alive.   Puritan ministers and Bishops and divines visited her and consulted her.   She wrote several pious books, and when she died there was no limit to the extravagant eulogies passed on her.   The funeral sermon by Antony Walker entitled " The virtuous woman found " was printed.   The pious meditations with which she fills her diary are in the common form, taught no doubt by the divines of the day, many of whom visited Leighs.   Her almost daily practice was to go " into the wilderness to meditate."   This was a wild part of the garden and she tells her " usual time " for this occupation was two hours.   In fact, she revelled like so many others in all forms of self-humiliation and supplication, and her diary, kept between 1666 and 1677, was written for disciplinary purposes and re-read so that she might groan and groan again over her past sins.

I spent much time in reading in some of my Diarys of some years before whilest I was doing so I found God mightily upon my spirit both wearing and melting my heart and making me shed a great plenty of tears.

She is " large in confessing ye great vanity " of her youth and deplores having spent " mӯ precious time in reading romances in seeing and reading plays in dressing and adorning my vile body in looking glasses to set out myself," also

" in curious dressing in playing cards " and " my disobedience to my father."

This last seems to show that she regretted not having
married the other man.   This conjecture is borne out by the
very frequent entries in which her husband is referred to.
For there can be no question that Mary was not happy with
him.   Of course we have only the diarist's version of the
trouble.   Charles Rich, Earl of Warwick, used bad language.
If Mary's conversation was anything like the style of her
diary we forgive him at once, more than this we find an
excuse for him.   Moreover, the unfortunate man was often
tortured by gout.   But a wife who according to her own
account prayed privately and publicly " pants and breaths "
after it, fasted, wept continually over her own sins, thought
and spoke constantly of death, lectured the servants and
also her husband, was often engaged in holy intercourse
with divines and was famous for performing " considerable
works of charity " must have been difficult to live up to.
But there can be no question of Mary's sincerity.   She confesses faults of temper inherited no doubt from her dictatorial
and noble father.   So far as the diary is concerned these
entries with regard to her husband do much to relieve what
would otherwise be an unquotable torrent of piety.

At first it is only hot argument :

when I had supt my Lord was out of humor and disputed with great
passion with me and did so provoke me that I was surprised into a
sudden disputing with him contrary to my resolution and tho' I said
nothing but what was with respect to him yet his fierceness made me
troubled that I had disputed with him afterwards past it over and
committed myself to God in prayer.

She prays for him and talks to him.   He listens with
patience.   She notes that she bewails her " husband's swearing."   Her brother-in-law, Hatton, at dinner " did dreadfully swear and talk so very ill that I thought nothing out
of Hell could have done."   She is obliged to retire because
this brings on a bad attack of swearing from her husband.
Later again " My Lord was passionate with me without any
occasion and shot out his arrows even bitter words," and it
becomes pathetic when she tells him " that I was with his

unkindness to me so much troubled that I was weary of my
Life." There are times when he listens to her and coming
home one day from a visit she impresses on him " how much
thankfulness we ow'd to God who had given us such sweet
parks and sweet accommodations." This time he does not
swear ; but not very long passes before he is at it again, at
dinner too before guests. She waits till they are gone, and
then bursts into tears. Sometimes she is able to bear it
" without returning railing for railing," but at other times
her own temper is too much for her :

After dinner was tending my Lord towards even without any great
occasion given me I found a sudden eruption of my passions and
found them make great work within me making me very furious and
much disordered and tho' I did not break out before the company
into any passionate speeches or speak one word or had any notice
taken of my disorder yet when I came alone I spoke passionate
words to myself w^h tho' none other did hear yet O Lord thou didst.

Had this afternoon with my L. dispute wherein I was confidant I
was in ye right but he in ye dispute growing violently passionate I
still inconsiderately held on ye dispute which made him in his passion
break forth most bitterly.

One day begins by some good discourse with him, but
ends in his having an outbreak of swearing when she persists
about something—she finds him " in an extraordinary manner
provoking." When he dies in 1673, after a long illness, she
commits her thoughts to " Ye Round Book." She says in
the diary, however, that she is " much opprest and extremely
saded " by the loss. But we cannot help thinking it must
have been something of a relief to her.

Mary did not live, as one might suppose, the life of a religious recluse. She goes to London, dines with the Ld. Chamberlain, Lady Albemarle and others, visits her sisters Lady
Ranelagh and Lady Goring and goes to Court. But she is
always delighted to return to " Leez " so as " to enjoy more
communion with God " :

I was much pleased that I was now retiring to my quiet home from
Ye hurry I had been in at London. I had this consolation that I
could truly say I never found my heart taken with any worldly pomp
or vanity I had seen there.

There is a touch of self-righteousness about this and the following :

Had this day at dinner my Lo Maynard and Col. Talbot. I heard from them much vain discourse but my heart did not close with it but abhorr'd it.

Shopping makes her " dull and distracted in prayer," but her heart is " not at all affected with ye court."

Occasionally she notes public events such as :

Towards evening came ye news of London being on fire which amazed me and troubled me.

But for the most part her object seems to have been to keep a store of penitential and supplicatory reflections and her religious intercourse with the various divines. There is a " holy Mr. Warren," and " Mr. Woodrooffe," as well as these mentioned in the following typical entry :

In ye morning I got Mr. Colly to pray with me at dinner and till even had a great many of my godly neighbors come to see me with whom I had a great deal of good discourse, Mr. Lavendore did much move me by his holy discourse. After supper I got Mr. Walker to pray with me in my closet I was somewhat dull and sleepy in that prayer yet my heart did breath after God.

She died in 1678. The MS. of the Diary is in the British Museum (MS. 27351–55) and selections written out by Woodroofe (MS. 27358).

ELIZABETH FREKE

"MRS. ELIZABETH FREKE her diary 1671 to 1714 some few remembrances of my misfortunes which have attended me in my unhappy life since I were marryed wch was November the 14. 1671."

This is the title of the tale of woe and grumbling which constitutes Elizabeth Freke's truly astonishing diary. Her determination to pose as a martyr is kept up to the end. From her own account she must have been an impossible woman, and although we only have her side of the story we can quite understand why her husband stayed with her so little and why every one quarrelled with her. Nevertheless, her record is extremely amusing.

The first few years are retrospective and the entries are few in each year. Later she writes more frequently but never every day. She evidently wanted to detach the " misfortunes " and sorrows, and to leave the quieter and more happy days unrecorded. Every entry is signed " Eliz. Freke." Attached to the Diary is a complete inventory of her furniture, some " receits of cakes, sweetmeats etc " and " a table of phisycall receits."

She begins by relating her ancestry and her marriage to her cousin Percy Freke. He was her cousin, a son of Captain Arthur Freke of Rathbury Castle, Co. Cork. He was a spendthrift who squandered what money he could get in acquiring more land in Ireland. At one time he was Member for Clonakilty. She married him, she tells us, on " a most dreadfull, Raynie day, A presager of all my sorrows and Misfortunes to me." She records the birth of her son and her journeys to Ireland where throughout her husband seems to have taken refuge from her as he was interested in his property there. The only person for whom she expresses affection and devotion is her father, from whom she says she never had " one unkind word." He gives her money, although, in spite of her complaints, she never seems to have been really badly off :

A greatt Allteration itt was To whatt I found In Ireland from a Husband, And on my looking a Little Malloncally on some past Reflections, my dear Father Fancyed Itt was my Wantt of Mony and without saying A word to me went up into his Closett And Brought me downe presently In two Baggs under his Coate, Two hundred pounds which £200 hee charged me to keep privatt from my husband's knowledge and buy Needles and Pins with Itt.

He dies while she is away in Ireland at the age of eighty-nine to her " gret loss, Grife and unspeakable sorrow." Although she seems to have had plenty of houses to live in, she is always complaining that she has no " place to putt my unhappy Head in." Some instances of her troubles may be given—of illness and an accident :

I Fell downe quite sicke att my dear Sister Austins of A Malignant Feaver called by the name of the Plague Feaver and which Rained much in London and Abundance dyed of Itt. Those thatt lived were Marked By Itt and of which I kept my Bed Like to dye for neer two Month under the hands of the Docctors, Apothicarys & Surgions. After two month this Feaver Fell In to my Left side And settled in my Foot And Ankle as Blacke as A Cole wher Ill I lay of itt not Able to stirr in my Bed for Neer three month more all Concluding it would kill me But outt of this and my other Afflicttions (And my husband neer three years from me) my Greatt And good God after all delivered mee And Raised mee up Againe a Miserable specttle to know more of his Mercyes.

I came to London December the 5 to my dear sister Austins In Plumbtree Street where the very next day I fell down Right sicke And soe stufft up with A Tissick thatt I could hardly Fetch my Breath or goe Cross my Chamber or doune A paire of staires. . . .

I went up Into my uper Closett of an errant to fetch down six pound to pay Scerry the Mason for new Tileing part of the Hall blowne downe by the late Hurrycane & Wind ; when Coming Downe the second paire of staires my Head was soe taken thatt I Fell from the topp allmost to the Bottom, neer Twenty high staires, which, as Itt stun'd me soe for a Time I were as Dead, till Mr Freke (heering the Noise of my Fall & noe Complaintt) Made A shift to gett out of his Bed, who had nott bin outt of Itt in 6 weeks befor, In his shirt (Aboutt nine A clock in the Morning) knocked and Called Company to him & I were by Fowre Men taken up allmost Dead, & Laid on A Bed ; my head and Face soe Battered Against the Wall, My Back to all Judgment all most Brok against the Stairs & the Cupp of my Left knee Brok. The voylence of this my Fall struck outt my Cheek Teeth thatt, strong as they weer, Fell outt of my Mouth—Roots and all—into my hand and brok outt my other Teeth.

As may be imagined, the consequence of this appalling accident occupy many subsequent entries. There are occasional attempts at reconciliation with her husband, who says that he will live with her " for that he found Friends were but Indifferent Cementers Between Man & wife," and in spite of her constant complaints against him she often refers to him as " my deer Husband." Her journeys to Ireland were not without incident as the following description shows :

Wee were all Like to be Lost by most Tempestyous Wynds and Raine, butt, by Gods Mercy, we putt In att Illford Combe where I stayed Sunday, Monday & Tuesday & A Wensday by Two of the Clock in the Morning, the 28 of August, the wind Changed, & I wentt with Mr. Frek to sea Againe, & Came thatt Night within A Watch of Reaching Watterford ; Butt on A suden, aboutt sunsett thatt Nightt, the Wynd Changed, with The Most hidious Tempest of Wynd & Raine, wch brought us Back againe next day att Nightt to Lundy, wher we Lay with 4 ships more, dispairing of Life, with our Mast all downe, our Cabin shutt upp, & our Anchors Lost. We Lay roleing till nextt night, when being In a despratt Condition, we A Tempted to shoot the Bay of Barstable, wher all that saw us on the Hill gave us over for Lost. Butt by Gods greatt Mercy wee safe Landed att Barstable. About sunsetting, wher wth Captaine Jeffryes, we staid A weeke Till Aboutt September the 5, when we wentt to Sea Againe, & by Gods Mercy to me, wee all Landed safe In Cork Harbour, tho' persued by severall Algeriens, Septem. 6. i677. For which Mercy the Greatt God Make me ever thankfull, & Grant I May Never forgett his Goodness to me whilst I am Elizabeth Freke.

Mr. Freke escapes from a fatal accident in which it will be noted the chair he was sitting in is the cause of her chief concern :

About Wednesday August the thirtieth Mr. Frek sitting in A Chaire by my Greatt Barne doore to see A Load of Barley goe into the Barne, I was butt Just Gone from him (I think for a couchin for him) And the horses very gentle ; without any provocation, the Cartt In the Twinkling of an Eye Run Itt selfe full against that Chaire Mr. Freke was sitting In & Broke Itt all to Bitts, To the A Mazement of All that saw Itt ; and A new Chaire too.

Mr. Freke escaped behind the barn door just in time. Whatever her feelings towards her husband may have been, his prolonged illness from dropsy gives her many an opportunity for writing heart-rending details describing how she sees " my dear Husband Murdered by Five Doctors two Surgions & three Apothycarys." While watching over him she is attacked by the " Curratt " and another man " both of Them Drunke & Like to Beasts & Called me Crassy woman." When he dies " Noe Mortall was with him butt my wretched selfe " and " my A mazed condition was such as my crying out soon filled the house." She gives him a very expensive funeral " suiteable to his Quality and desertt " which cost her above eleven hundred and fifty pounds. The death of her grandchild took place earlier in the same year. She describes it as

the most fatallest thing ever Hapned to mee & I shall Lamentt Itt for I had sett my whole hartt on Him Which itt has brok, thatt & me, for any comfort in this Life.

She again falls down stairs on another occasion when luckily sister Austin, who was at the foot of the stairs, broke her fall.

After the removal of her husband one feels there may be some mitigation of the lamentations. But far from it. She goes on quarrelling with her son and daughter-in-law, she is thrown out of her carriage because the Coachman is drunk, she has " longe Fitts of Tissick " and other painful illnesses, receives dismal accounts of her Irish estates, discharges her chaplain for his " deBauchory," suffers " an Infinite sortt of Loses and Troubles " from her tenants, is worried by law-suits, receives no help from her cousin from whom she gets " very rough letters " and no " humanity " from her sister, has several bad disputes about her timber, suffers the loss of a coach mare which was " stole from me," wrangles with the Bishop's Chancellor who " Gahezy-like Tormented me with his proctters and Baylyes," is " taken with A Multitude of Black Flyes In my eyes which I never had before in my life did Almost take Away my sight," enumerates the sums of money she gave to her dear sister Austin who nevertheless leaves her because she " would not beare my Malloncholly one winter," is attacked by " two Great Rogues of Baylyes " who search her room, has her Barns blown down by a storm and while

sitting in my Chamber All Alone Reading some partt of my Will, when on A suden my head Catchtt all A Fire and In three minits Time burntt all my head Cloths Close to my haire ; And I being all A Lone could nott gett them off or any body to me, thatt Itt was God's greatt Mercy I was nott Burntt to death and I doe humbly thank him for itt.

This would seem to be enough, but it still goes on ; her kitchen chimney falls down and she is nearly burnt, four of her servants conspire to murder her, she only receives one letter from her son in three years, her cousin John loses his temper with her, in London she is confined to her Chair for two months, at the age of seventy she is " not able the least to help myselfe butt assisted by Two of my servants and noe friend Neer me butt all Cheats," the doctor bloods her for pleurisy and as usual she has " noe Frind Neer mee," two of her servants steal, she makes a complaint and the Justice

ordered them both a good whiping and what further I pleased which I saw done to them both outt of my window Att the Carts Taile 27 May Satterday, Till the Blood spun for example's sake.

She gains much satisfaction from the truly appalling punishments which the Almighty inflicts on her enemies :

Butt to God I made my Complaint Who signally Lett me see his Justice & Goodness to me, In the fall of my enimise, For soon affter he Came from the Asises, one of Turners eyes dropt outt of his head on his Book, and Aboutt three Month Affter his Wiffe dyed from him, Raveing, And nott Long affter God Took him a Way to Accountt for his Perjury.   And his son in Law, Captain Asdall thatt Marryed his only daughter, Run Away to the West Indies with Another Wife, and all this In the Compass of Little more than half A yeare, as I foretold him by my Letter ; Itt was Revealed to me from Above. And for Henry Towrs, my other perjuered oath man, soon affter he came home, he dyed sudenly & sencelessly & was privatly putt in the Ground for fear of A worse Accident to him, by Nine A Clock in the Morning, and these things Looked to me like something of A Judgment on him. Besids Mr Towrs eldest son, A Livetenantt, poysoned himself to Avoyd the Justice of the Law, whene he was

Arained & Condemned by A Courtt Marshall for selling his souldiers to France, with Captain Somes & Dashwood, who all three poysoned themselves. Iff this does nott look like A Judgment &c. I know nott whatt does; & I humbly thank God I am still A Live, and see justice from the hand of God to my enimies.

Her son married Elizabeth, daughter of Sir John Meade, of Ballintobber, Co. Cork. They " being desirous of more Quality " she buys them the patent of a baronetcy, but she gets no thanks and refers to his children as a " Rude family." So it goes on with almost ceaseless grumbling to the end, two months before her death. It is only fair to say that there is now and then occasional—though very rare—relief, as for instance :

This New Years day I had according to old custom all my Tennants dine with me, with near Twenty dishes of Meatt and what Ale and Brandy they please to drink with Cards butt noe Musicke.

In one part of the Diary she writes out " An account of what Bottles I have now In my uper Closetts, of Cordiall Waters and Sirups ; put in by me Eliz. Frek for my own usc." The list comprises over 250 bottles, including amongst others " Aquamirabolus, Buckthorn sirrup, Popywater, Redstrek Cider, Cowslipp Wyne, Damson Wyne, White Meade, & Elder Vinegar." She records making several rather lavish gifts to the Church. There is also an inventory of her furniture which is a most elaborate long document giving the contents of every room, the furniture, plate, books and pictures. Among the latter " one long picture of my wretched selfe " and among the furniture " 1 coffin for me and Itts stands Redy Fixtt and Leaded for me with key of vault."

It is impossible to resist quoting some of her 446 prescriptions :

To stay Bleeding att the Nose.
Tye the Lower Joynte of the Little finger with a purple Silk very hard ; or a drye Toad hung aboute the Neck, or a piece of Cloth diped in Vinegar, burnt, and snuff up the powder or Perriwinkle between ye Teeth.

Elks claw or hoof are a soveraiyne Remidy for the Falling sickness tho butt worn in a Ring much more taken inwardly ; but saith Mizaldus Itt must be the hoof of the Right foot Behinde.

The Head of a Young Kitte, being Burntt to Ashes and the quantity of A dragme taken every morning in a Little water is an admirable remedy against the Goute.

Judging by her correspondence, much of which is transcribed in her diary, by her lists, inventories, accounts and receipts, by her verses and notes on public events, Elizabeth Freke must have been a very capable, masterful woman. She probably had a bad temper, was intensely disagreeable, and suffered acutely from a persecution complex in which her imagination worked freely. She was buried in Westminster Abbey on the 12th of April, 1714.

One copy of the diary she wrote on large manuscript paper which she bound herself in a piece of the newly invented wall-paper. The second version is inscribed in a large folio volume bound in white vellum which her husband, knowing her weakness for MS. books, had given her in 1684, just before he left for Ireland.

The Diary, edited by Mary Carbery, was published in 1913, and also appeared in the collection of the Cork Archæological Society. This journal does not show how unfortunate she was but how she revelled in misfortune. Nevertheless, she must have impressed her personality very strongly on those around her, for even at the beginning of this century her name was well known in the village of West Bilney. Her old coach remained to the middle of the nineteenth century in the great Barn. Children who played round it could be frightened away with the cry, " Take care, Madam Freke will have you," and many legends of her tyranny survived.

ROWLAND DAVIES

THERE is a group of diaries connected with the Jacobite war at the end of the seventeenth century. Unfortunately none of them are very good. Ensign Cramond's [1] and Bonnivert's [2] are merely scraps. John Stevens [3] left a record which he wrote up from daily notes and corrected for publication. Stevens was a Catholic and ardent Jacobite who fled to France in 1689 ; he made many translations of Spanish books and did some archæological work. His style is literary and curiously modern and in addition to military notes he gives social and topographical information. But as a diary there is nothing in this production which merits special quotation. Then there is the diary of William King [4] who eventually became Archbishop of Dublin, which has already been noted. The best of the group from the point of view of diary writing is that of the Rev. Rowland Davies, who ended his days as Dean of Cork. He kept a daily diary in 1689 and 1690. Although it is matter of fact and rather bald, he tells us something of himself and gives a description as an eye-witness of the campaign in Ireland. When James landed in Ireland Rowland Davies came over to England with other Irish Protestants. He served at Camberwell where Dr. Parr was vicar. Many entries, therefore, describe his visits to London. He is present at William and Mary's coronation which was "very sumptuous." William "looked very brisk and cheerful and the Queen abundantly more." He visits Evelyn at Deptford :

[1] Add. MS. 29878.   [2] 1038 B.M.
[3] *The Journal of John Stevens*, ed. by Robert Murray (1912).
[4] See p. 18.

" there saw his gardens and varieties of trees, with several rareties, and also drank some quince wine. He also assured me that the best time to remove any greens was in August or in the spring and that yew grows as readily and easily from a slip as rosemary being either twisted or bruised before it is set.

While he is of a studious disposition

I spent this day at Camberwell in very close study without conversing with any person

and is conscientious about his sermons, he visits the theatre, plays at cards (but not for high stakes, losing only sixpence after several hours' play) and attends a wrestling match :

After dinner we had a famous bout of wrestling between Dantor, a shoemaker of Ireland, and one Burton, a printer and I won a bottle of wine on the latter's head.

He tells us of the clothes he buys, spending on one occasion as much as nine pounds eight shillings. He also purchases " a mole tippet." But his manners apparently left something to be desired as he is " sharply reprehended " by his landlady at Camberwell " for spitting about the house."

There must have been some pretty sights in the London of those days. Coming up from Camberwell one day he says :

I saw also this day many milkmaids dancing in the streets with their pails upon their heads dressed with garlands and hung with plate of great value.

Rowland Davies, before he took priest's orders, was trained for the medical profession. His notes therefore on his own health and the prescriptions he gives to invalids are technical and professional. A few entries may be given in full showing how closely concerned this reverend gentleman was with the spiritual and physical welfare of the people of Yarmouth, where he held a lectureship for a short time.

Mr. Milbourn read prayers and I preached, Corinthians xv. 33. After noon I read prayers ; christened six children. Mr Milbourn preached. Then I visited Mr Taylor whom I found in a dying condition his stomach being imposthumated and swoln very high. I prayed with him, and in order to abate his pain ordered a fomentation of bitter herbs to be applied which answered my expectation, but he died that night. I visited Mr. Ferrier also and found him complaining the sickness in his stomach but would not take any more than four doses of the *cortex*. In the evening I found Mrs. Patty still delirious. I ordered her abdomen to be fomented with an hysterical decoction then gave her thirty drops of *ipec.* in an hysteric julep whereon she took some rest.

I visited Mrs Pew and prayed with her and appointed the next morning to give her the sacrament ; as I came away her husband put a crown piece into my hand. Then I went to Mr. Godfrey's where I dined ; there I heard an account of the Turks being defeated. After dinner I visited Mr. Ferrier and he complaining of sickness in his stomach, a fomentation of bitter herbs I directed for him ; I ordered also a clyster for Mrs Patty and a plaster to her poll which caused a great blister, but her distemper altered not by it. I also waited on the bailiffs and gave them intimation of my design to return to London, that they might provide accordingly.

About four in the morning on the change of the moon, Mrs. Patty fell into violent convulsions whereon I was called and Dr. Cotton sent for. By the time he came she appeared to be apologetic whereon I had her cupped on each shoulder which brought her a little to her senses. Then the doctor advised an application of pigeons to her head, which made some fermentation and disorder ; but she came not to herself all day, but, her pulse being vermicular and all other symptoms ill, I despaired of anything but death suddenly. I went to Church. As usual Mr. Milbourn read prayers and I preached in the morning Luke xviii. 14 and in the afternoon I read prayers and baptized seven children and he preached in the evening. That evening I spent at home.

The reader may be interested to learn that Mrs. Patty, after further drastic treatment, eventually recovered. Rowland Davies finds time for an occasional dance and supper parties, but his thoughts become more and more preoccupied by events in Ireland, which he records in his entries from time to time. At last he obtains an appointment as chaplain to one of the regiments which accompanied King William in May, 1690. He was present at the Boyne, the siege of Limerick and through the whole Irish campaign. The success which attended the royal arms at the siege of Cork appears to have been facilitated by his knowledge of the locality. But the overshadowing importance of the events

9

in which he participates caused a complete change in the style of his diary and needless to say it does not improve it. Instead of observations on trivial events of the day, we get an elaborate military chronicle. Although a chaplain he shows in the purchase of his equipment that he had no intention of being a non-combatant. He buys " a carbine, a sword, a bayonet, a horse holster cap and furniture, etc.," and makes a further purchase of another sword and " other arms." He relates the King's escape on the eve of the battle :

At two in the morning we decamped again and marched towards Drogheda where we found King James encamped on the other side of the Boyne ; we drew up all our horses in a line opposite him within cannon shot, and as his Majesty passed our line they fired six shots at him one whereof fell and struck off the top of the Duke of Warternberg's pistol and the whiskers off his horse and another tore the King's coat on the shoulder. We stood open during at least twenty shot until, a man and two horses being killed among the Dutch guards, we all retired into a trench behind us, where we lay safe while much mischief was done to other regiments and in the evening drew off and encamped behind the hill.

Only an extract can be given from his long entry describing the Battle of the Boyne :

His Majesty then came up and charged at the head of the Enniskilling horse, who deserted him at the first charge and carried with them a Dutch regiment that sustained them ; but the King's blue troop of guards soon supplied this place, and with them he charged in person and routed the enemy, and coming over the hill near Duluk appeared on our flank and, being not known at first, made all our forces halt and drew up again in order, which gave the enemy time to rally also, and draw up on the side of the hill, a bog and river being between us, and then they fired two pieces of cannon on us, but did no mischief ; but as soon as our foot and cannon came up, they marched on, and we after them, but, our foot being unable to march as they did, we could not come up to fight again, but, the night coming on were forced to let them go ; but had we engaged half an hour sooner or the day held an hour longer, we had certainly destroyed that army.

We hear very little of his duties as chaplain except on one occasion when he preaches against swearing. The diary ceases on September 30, 1690.

Rowland Davies, established in Ireland after the war, eventually became Dean of Cork and occupied his time in writing controversial religious books. He died in 1721.

The Journal was printed by the Camden Society in 1857.

JOHN SCOTT

PART of a diary (1704 to 1708) kept by a young divinity
student of Donaghadee gives the story of a love affair
which subsequent events prove was unsuccessful.
John Scott was the son of Captain Matthew Scott, mariner,
of Donaghadee. He was licensed in 1707 by the Down
Presbytery to the General Synod of Ulster to preach the
Gospel. Beyond his diary that is all that is known of him.
He writes punctually. When he has nothing to say he puts,
" I was domi p. diem." For one week this is the only entry
every day. We can gather that he was a young man of
some spirit by an early entry in 1704 :

" Fraiday 15th December I was att home and in company w^th
my father who was same day under Physick, when Hugh Campbell
wth Wm. Pinkstane came to my father wth his Bill of Cost : presented
it, & after some time, he was provoked, tho' no cause was given, to
give my father a blow, whereupon I gott up, gott him in my arms &
desired him to be sober, and att length gott him pulled from my
father and then interposing betwixt them quieted him, he made towards
my father the second time, I again interveans & desires him to give
me the blow & not meddle with father, & so I gives him a blow w^th
my fist on the face he was afterward pretty sober, only told me he
would give me a blow another time, and promising the same elsewhere namely Pinkstan's in the audience of Capt. Montgomery, Jo^n
Mc Cormick of Newry & Arch Milling he was indeed as good as his
word, for same night Fraiday 15th he came in Street door & chamber
door being open ; & as he entered the room door he drew his oak
cudgel, wth this expression, were you not a base villan to beat me
so in the morning & so let drive att me, but ever blessed be my God,
who at all times safeguards his own, destined one of the beams of
the house to receive it from me, & when it was over, namely, the
blow, I clapt in to him & gott hold on him and att length gott him
under me, and so beat him wth my fists untill I was allmost weary,
and at last I gott him put out of the house, & while att the door &

chamber window he threatened to put me from preaching & to burn the house upon us.

The following entries show his ordinary pursuits :

Wensday 14th March I was att no sermon the Sabbath before Mr. Hamilton had given intimation that there would be no weak days sermon because of the sowing.

Teusday 17th April I went to Belfast and bought a hatt price 5s: 10d and two yards & 3 quarters of broad-cloath at 5 as I judge it may be, because it was not paid them p yeard. I returned same night.

Wensday 15th August I heard Mr. Hamilton on Jon 4 : 2 & was domi p diem. Memorandum that same day I went to Tho: Wrights who was going to my father to Dublin & gave him the Key of my father's chest & at my return I overheard Janet Barkley cursing Jon Blair whom I reproved . . . I was a little out of humour through her & she was pleased to declare throughout the town that I abused her when God knows it was the glory of God & the good of her poor soul that I designed by the reproof by me reached her, but I fear poor woman she is given up of God.

Saturday 8th June, I slept till near 4 in the afternoon [1] about 5 it was noised through the town that the Meeting house was on fire, as soon as I got my shooses on my feet & my coat on my back, I ran as fast thither as possibly I could and found true what was noised, but blessed be God it was soon quenched, so that it did not much harm, the occasion of it was Jamie allen the coll[rs] son his firing a musquet at a bird that was upon the house, and the weather being dry & the forrage of the gun carring to the thatch set it on fire by him not designed I am persuaded.

Munday 20th September I was in Donoghadee it being a fair day. I was some time with Mr. Ja. Hamilton in Ja. Kennedy's & Ja. Hay's, God pardon the sin of mispending time, precious time. Memorandum Mr James Hamilton sent with Mitchel to Ed[r] for a perriwig about five and twenty or thirty shillings price. Mitchel was to return within 6 weeks.

Teusday 15th April I went to Belfast and bought as much black cloath 8 shil p yeard as made me a coat viz. 2 yeards and $\frac{1}{2}$ & $\frac{1}{2}$ quarter black cloath from Tho Lyle I also bought as much serge dinnim as was for bretches. I also bought a hat price being 6 Shill. ster. Memorandum that I heard at that time Mr David Thome preach in Belfast meeting-house on these words work out your

[1] He had been riding from Antrim all night before.

salvation wth fear & trembling. I came to Donnoghadee same night.

The Rev. Henry Hamilton of Donaghadee had a daughter Jean. John Scott fell in love with her and refers to her as " domina " or " doa." The affair begins in 1705 when he writes that he went down to Mr. Hamilton " where I was for some space of time wth the mistris." In 1707 the affair becomes serious and he sometimes writes about it in Latin, putting in English words when he is at a loss. A series of these entries may be given (with a translation of the Latin ones), for his devotion to Jean became his main preoccupation :

Saturday 1st November I was in Donaghadee about eleven o'clock. I went to Mr Hamilton's and met in the entrance Mrs. Jean, to whom I had spoken and she promised to meet me about 6 o'clock near the church. At that time I disclosed to her what was in my mind, and to console me she said that she would think over the matter about which I had spoken. I was with her about two hours and we separated near the church.

I at my return went down to Mr Hamilton's went in and meet Doâ in armatorio, where about the space of an hour I was wth her and had indeed a desirable time tho' still very nice.

In the evening went down to Mr Hamilton's and met Dôâ in the small room, where I was with her for six or seven hours—father and mother in Belfast.

I was in the evening in Mr Hamilton's and took occasion to signify to Mrs. Hamilton quam maximum amorem I had for Dôâ Janâ ejus filiâ she told me she would not be my foe but rather my friend, for wch I returned her many thanks. I was for some time at the Turf stack same night cum Dôâ.

I came home and about 9 of the clock I went down and meet wth Dôâ I was illa cum circitur semi horam et illae dedi Gloves. (I was with her about half an hour and gave her gloves).

In the evening I was about 2 hours wth Dôâ from whome I had the following encouragement for Wednesday the 19 of 9ber I expected a reply to what I had some time before proposed to her : wch was that if she did not alter she would accept of and in due time reward my service ; but if she altered then she was to be free.

I went down before daylight to Mr Hamilton's and was cum Dôâ in the guest chamber from 7 of the clock till near 9. I was wth

her from half eleven till $\frac{1}{2}$ three in the afternoon ; in the evening I just saw her she being bussied making a furbelow'd skerf in order to go to Mrs Mair's Dorothy Hamilton's burial. I gave, memorandum, to Isabel a handkerchief and pair of gloves.

I was in Donnoghadee and in the evening went down to Mr Hamilton's, and was with Dôâ in her closet from 6 to 10 of the clock. I did same night present her wth a little bottle ; she was pleased by her carriage towards me to evidence more concernedness for me and love to me than ever formerly.

There is a hitch because **Mr. Hamilton** considers that Scott's father should have spoken to him. Mrs. Hamilton, however, is very favourable and all seems to be arranged satisfactorily :

I was domi p diem, only in the evening I went down to Mr Hamilton's and was with Dôâ in the guest chamber from six of the clock to nine, my father did same night to Mr Hamilton make known the respect I had for his daughter Mrs Jean ; and his reply to him was that he would give me his daughter to wife, rather yea and sooner than to many wth 400 p annum wherewith my father was mightily taken ; and indeed no wonder for it was much more than he was expecting and looking for from him.

And when his father is ill Jean pays him a visit and certainly appears to give him every encouragement.

Sabbath 14th March I was in D.dee and in the morning was taken wth a pain in my head wch did obleidge me to keep my room, about ten I went to bed, resolving to sweat for it, the wch I did vehemently till 8 at night. Memorandum that same day about 1 in the afternoon my father was seized wth the gravel and continued most violent to 6 of the clock Munday's night about 7 of the clock at night Mr McCracken Mr Hamilton Mrs Hamilton & my Dear Mrs Jean came to see my father who then was much tormented Dôâ came to the back of the bed to me where I had occasion to see and speak wth her and had from her 3 oscula (three kisses) wch were at that time to me very refreshing.

After a few more entries of the same kind the record ends. It comes, therefore, as a blow to learn that John never married Jean. Five years later she married a widower, the Rev. Robert Gordon of Rathfriland, who, curiously enough, married as his third wife John Scott's sister Esther.

This diary is a good instance of a fragment which gives

us an unexplained and pathetic incident and leaves us wondering.

The successful Robert Gordon kept a sort of family record,
entering the births of his twenty-five children with great
exactitude. It would appear, as Mr. Stevenson [1] says, that
some of the infants came into the world with labels bearing
their names attached :

My dear wife was delivered of a son called Hamilton.

My dear wife was delivered of a daughter called Isabell

He writes a eulogy of Jean when she dies, but this leaves
us cold after her behaviour to John Scott.   He also inserts a
memorandum on his escape from death after drinking milk
and beer mixed.   Dr. Rutty, it will be remembered, after
drinking cyder and whisky, wrote " tremble at the mixture," [2]
but " the terrors of death " did not " cease upon " him, as
was the case with the Reverend Robert.   Jean's husband,
however, was not a diarist.   Her lover was.

The manuscript of Scott's diary was in the possession of
the late Dr. James F. St. John Annesley and quotations from
it are given in *Two Centuries of Life in Down*, by John Stevenson (1920).

[1] *Two Centuries of Life in Down.*
[2] *English Diaries*, p. 217.

SWIFT

THE Journal to Stella might be regarded merely as a collection of letters. But the form of it, with its punctual daily entries, gives it all the character of a diary. Moreover, each day is freshly recorded on that day and no diary reflects the passing temper and whim of the moment more vividly than this famous Journal. There are other instances of diaries being addressed to a particular person. This makes the motive of the diarist perfectly plain. He writes for a particular eye ; he writes to be read in a few days. We may thus be deprived of the usual mystery of the uncertain intention of the author in keeping a diary at all, and we cannot expect introspection and self-examination, nor, as we shall see, complete honesty. In fact, the diary necessarily becomes objective and self-conscious. Nevertheless, it reflects mood and personality in the daily examination of passing events both great and small.

Sir Walter Scott describes the Journal to Stella in his edition of Swift's works and says it is " as unconstrained as conversation." Swift, he says, wrote " without coldness or suspicion, with all the intimacy of a husband but with all the feelings of a lover. Nothing was too precious to be withheld from her and at the same time nothing too trifling in which she was not to find interest if it related to him. Hence that curious and diverting mixture of the meanest and most common domestic details with State secrets, Court intrigues and the fate of ministries ; where the history of the Duke of Marlborough's disgrace is hardly detailed with more minute accuracy than the progress and cure of the doctor's broken shin."

The Journal was written between September, 1710 and June, 1713. Swift, although born in Dublin, was of English family, but it is quite unnecessary to give any biographical notice of so famous a figure.   His original object in going to London, where the Journal was written, was to solicit on behalf of the Bishops of Ireland that Queen Anne would be pleased to remit the right of the crown to the firstfruits and twentieth parts payable by the clergy of that kingdom. But this soon became a very subordinate occupation and he settled down to enjoy the society in which he found he was very welcome and to associate with all the prominent people of the day.   He was in a position, therefore, to pick up a great deal of gossip and to take part in the various political and social intrigues of the time.   He wrote his journal every day and sent it when he had covered a certain amount of paper.   In his notes he addressed his correspondents as M.D. chiefly ;   sometimes D or D.D.   For caution's sake Mrs. Dingley is addressed as well as Stella (Mrs. Johnson) and the initials refer to one or both of them.   PDFR stands for himself, or sometimes " Presto."   The terms of endearment by which he often addresses them in the earlier part of the Journal are certainly very original.   " Sirrahs " occurs frequently and also " saucy little pretty dear rogues," " little monkies mine," " spiteful sluts," " dear saucy brats," " saucebox " and so on.   That Mrs. Dingley should be included for propriety's sake seems curious.   She was an unattractive lady who wore hinged spectacles and consumed large quantities of tobacco.

We get Swift's intention when he writes :

Henceforth I will write something everyday to MD and make it a sort of Journal, and when it is full, I will send it whether MD writes or not ; and so that will be pretty ; and I shall always be in conversation with MD and MD with Presto.

Later he asks :

Tell me do you like this journal way of writing ?   Is it not tedious and dull ?

Whatever they may have thought they could not have thought that.   It is certainly remarkable that this worldly, frivolous and cynical man should have so diligently and regu-

larly carried out his intention.   Except on account of illness
he hardly misses a day :

> Here is such a stir and bustle with this little MD of ours ;   I must
> be writing every night, I cannot go to bed without a word to them,
> I cannot put out my candle till I have bid them good night, O Lord,
> O Lord !

> Pshaw !   I must be writing to those dear saucy brats every night
> whether I will or no, let me have what business I will or come home
> ever so late or be ever so sleepy, but an old saying and a true one

> > Be you lords or be you earls
> > You must write to naughty girls.

This " old saying," like many others he quotes, was of
course invented by him on the spur of the moment.   Occasionally he writes in a coffee-house, but generally in bed at
night, " You must always write to your M Ds in bed, that is
a maxim."   It is in the little conversational introductions
and interludes which give the entries so much atmosphere
and make one accurately visualize the writer, tucked up in
bed, scribbling whatever came into his head.

> No faith you are just here upon this little paper and therefore I
> see and talk with you every evening constantly and sometimes in
> the morning.

> Well, I will leave you till I am got to bed and then I will say a
> word or two.
> Well it is now almost twelve and I have been busy ever since, by
> a fire too (I have my coals by half a bushel at a time, I will assure
> you)   And now I am got to bed.   Well and what have you to say
> to Presto now he is a bed ?   Come now, let us hear your speeches.
> No, it is a lie, I am not sleepy.   Let us sit up a little longer and talk.
> Well, where have you been today that you are but just this minute
> come home in a coach ?   What have you lost ?   Pay the coachman
> Stella. . . .

> You must understand Presto was sleepy and made blunders and
> blots.

> I am staying before I can fold up this letter till that ugly D is dry
> in the last line but one.   Do not you see it ?   O Lord I am loth to
> leave you, faith—but it must be so till next time.   Pox take that D.
> I will blot it to dry it.

Come come young women I keep a good fire ; it costs me twelve
pence a week and I fear something more ; vex me and I will have
one in my bedchamber too.   No, did not I tell you but just now, we
have no high winds here.   Have you forgot already ?   Now you
are at it again, silly Stella, why does your mother say my candles
are scandalous ?   they are good sixes in the pound and she said I
was extravagant enough to burn them by daylight.   I never burn
fewer at a time than one.

Seven morning.   I am rising to go to Jervas to finish my picture
and it is shaving day so good morrow M D ; but do not keep me
now for I cannot stay ; and pray dine with the dean but do not lose
your money.   I long to hear from you.   Ten at night.   I sat four
hours this morning for Jervas. . . .

These saucy jades take up so much of my time in writing to them.

They did not write to him nearly so often as he to them.
He describes receiving one of their letters :

who should come toward me but Patrick and gives me five letters
out of his pocket.   I read the superscription of the first, Pshah, said
I ;   and of the second, pshah, again ;   and of the third pshah, pshah,
pshah ;   and of the fourth, a gad, a gad, a gad I am in a rage ;   of the
fifth and last Ohoooa ;   ay marry this is something this is our M D so
truly we opened it, I think immediately and it began most impudently
in the world thus :   dear Presto, we are even thus far.   Now we are
even, quoth Stephen, when he gave his wife six blows for one.

There is a great deal of this amusing chaff and fooling, for
as he says " you must have chat and I must say every sorry
thing that comes into my head."   He uses the words of their
" little language " :   " gambling " for " rambling."   He is
" tosticated " between one place and another, and when the
frost breaks he says it is " very slabbery."   In one entry he
pretends that the Queen curtsies to him and " in a sort of
familiar way " asks after Stella.   Although he went to Court
he was never presented.   There was a question of his preaching to the Queen, but he did not like the prospect :

I hope they will forget it for if it should happen all the puppies
hereabouts will throng to hear me and expect something wonderful
and be plaguily balked ;   for I shall preach plain honest stuff.

However it never happened.   Here is Queen Anne at
Windsor :

There was a drawing room today at Court but so few company that the Queen sent for us into her bed chamber where we made our bows and stood about twenty of us round the room while she looked at us round with her fan in her mouth and once a minute said about three words to some that were nearest her and then she was told dinner was ready and went out.

Swift must have been an enormous social success. After the first three weeks he confesses : " It has cost me but three shillings in meat and drink since I came here." Although he started without birth, money or influence, it is not long before he worms himself into the inner councils of the great statesmen of the day. He sees a great deal of Harley and his friendship with Addison has its ups and downs. The Duke of Marlborough is referred to with a stinging cut on more than one occasion :

He is as covetous as Hell and ambitious as the Prince of it.

Of the Duchess he tells the following anecdote :

Lord-treasurer showed us a small picture enamelled work, and set in gold worth about twenty pounds ; a picture I mean of the Queen which she gave to the Duchess of Marlborough set in diamonds. When the Duchess was leaving England, she took off all the diamonds and gave the picture to one Mrs. Higgins (an old intriguing woman whom every body knows) bidding her make the best of it she could. Lord-treasurer sent to Mrs. Higgins for this picture and gave her a hundred pounds for it. Was ever such an ungrateful beast as that Duchess ? or did you ever hear such a story ? I suppose the Whigs will not believe it. Pray try them. She takes off the diamonds, and gives away the picture to an insignificant woman as a thing of no consequence ; and gives it to her to sell like a piece of old-fashioned plate. Is she not a detestable slut ?

Lord Peterborough is dismissed with " It is the ramblingest lying tongue on earth." An expression of sympathy comes for Lady Kerry, " we are so fond of one another because our ailments are the same." We catch a glimpse of William Penn :

Will Pen the Quaker at the head of his brethren to thank the duke for his kindness to their people in Ireland. To see a dozen scoundrels with their hats on and the Duke complimenting them with his off was a good sight enough.

The Journal shows one to what extent Swift was in request in all the great houses. He often plays " ombre," but not very successfully :

I lost my money at ombre sadly ; I make a thousand blunders at it. I play three penny ombre ; but it is what you call running ombre. Lady Clarges and a drab I hate won a dozen shillings of me last night.

He enjoys being in the very thick of it, revelling in the intrigues, yet sometimes in his disappointments wearying of the political machinations :

the Ministry all use me perfectly well and all that know them say they love me. Yet I can count upon nothing nor will but upon M D's love and kindness. They think me useful ; they pretended they were afraid of none but me ; and that they resolved to have me ; they have often confessed this yet all makes little impression upon me.

He refers to his wire-pulling with some pride but with bitterness at the absence of gratitude :

I met Mr Addison and pastoral Philips on the Mall today and took a turn with them ; but they both looked terribly dry and cold. A curse of party ! And do you know I have taken more pains to recommend the Whig wits to the favour and mercy of the Ministers than any other people. Steele I have kept in his place. Congreve I have got to be used kindly and secured. Rowe I have recommended and get a promise of a place. Philips I should certainly have provided for if he had not run party mad and made me withdraw my recommendation. I set Addison so right at first that he might have been employed and have partly secured him the place he has ; yet I am worse used by that faction than any man.

I'll tell you a good thing ; there is not one of the ministry but what will employ me, as gravely to speak for them to lord-treasurer, as if I were their brother or his ; and I do it as gravely ; though I know they do it only because they will not make themselves uneasy or had rather I should be denied than they.

As to actual politics. There is not very much of it :

I wonder I never write politics to you. I could make you the profoundest politician in all the land.

Well, but if you like them I will scatter a little now and then and mine are all fresh from the chief hands.

I tell you what comes into my head, that I never knew whether you were Whigs or Tories and I value our conversation the more that it never turned on that subject. I have a fancy that Ppt is a Tory and a rigid one. I don't know why ; but methinks she looks like one and D.D. a sort of trimmer. Am I right ?

No more than one specimen of a political entry need be given :

In my opinion we have nothing to save us but a peace and I am sure we cannot have such a one as we hoped and then the Whigs will bawl what they would have done had they continued in power. I tell the Ministry this as much as I dare and shall venture to say a little more to them especially about the Duke of Marlborough who as the Whigs give out will lay down his command ; and I question whether ever any wise state laid aside a general who had been successful nine years together whom the enemy so much dreaded and his own soldiers cannot but believe must always conquer ; and you know that in war opinion is nine parts in ten. The ministry leave me always with appearance of regard and much kindness ; but I doubt let personal quarrels mingle too much with their proceedings. Meantime they seem to value all this as nothing and are as easy and merry as if they had nothing in their hearts or upon their shoulders like physicians who endeavour to care but feel no grief whatever the patient suffers. Pshaw what is all this ? Do you know one thing, that I find I can write politics to you much easier than to anybody alive ? But I swear my head is full and I wish I were at Laracor with my dear chummy M D.

Swift was busy writing political tracts and other larger works. He often had difficulty in warding off visitors :

I toil like a horse and have hundreds of letters still to read : and squeeze a line out of each or at least the seeds of a line. Strafford goes back to Holland in a day or two and I hope our peace is very near. I have thirty pages more to write (that is to be extracted) which will be sixty in print. It is the most troublesome part of all, and I cannot keep myself private though I stole into a room up two pair of stairs when I came from Windsor ; but my present man has not yet learned his lesson of denying me discreetly.

But a few months later his man had improved :

You must know, I give chocolate almost every day to two or three people that I suffer to come to see me in the morning. My man begins to lie pretty well. Tis nothing for people to be denied ten times. My man knows all I will see and denies me to every body else.

Later in this same entry we get an idea of how he could make himself useful :

I was at court where everybody had their birthday clothes on and I dined with Lord-Treasurer who was very fine. He showed me some of the queen's speech which I corrected in several places and penned the vote of address of thanks for the speech.

His illnesses are very minutely described in the Journal, he tells his correspondents when he takes his pills, when he has a sore shin, the stages of his colds and perhaps the most graphic of all is his description of the shingles : " the flannel," " the Hungary water," the " urge urge urge ; dogs gnawing," the " cruel twinges," the spots, " now grown white and full of corruption," " prodigious hot and inflamed." Such an appeal for sympathy could not but be successful. This last illness seriously interferes with his daily writing and there is a long gap.

As the journal proceeds the frivolous note diminishes. He becomes concerned about his own future and when it finally gets to the point as to whether he is to be Dean of Windsor or of St. Patrick's, the entries are brief and businesslike.

His future fate—what sort of preferment he would get— was undoubtedly engaging his attention from the first. This comes out in the following entry in which another considera- tion appears which must also be discussed :

O faith I should be glad to be in the same Kingdom with M D, however although you were at Wexford. But I am kept here by a most capricious fate which I would break through if I could do it with decency or honour—To return without some mark of distinction would look extremely little ; and I would likewise gladly be some- what richer than I am. I will say no more but beg you to be easy till fortune take her course and to believe that M D's felicity is the great end I aim at in all my pursuits. And so let us talk no more on this subject which makes me melancholy and that I would fain divert. Believe me no man breathing at present has less share of happiness in life than I : I do not say I am unhappy at all but that everything here is tasteless to me for want of being where I would be.

Now there is plenty in the journal to show that Swift could combine cynicism and flippancy with warm feeling and true sympathy When Harley is stabbed, when a friend dies his expressions of grief and concern are genuine. Just as we feel annoyed at his worldliness we find him christening the coffeeman's child :

> This evening I christened our coffeeman Elliot's child ; where the rogue had a most noble supper and Steele and I sat among some scurvy company over a bowl of punch so that I am come home late, young women, and cannot stay to write to little rogues.

But in another connection we are confronted with an apparently serious though inevitable lack of candour. A reader of the Journal who knew nothing else whatever of Swift's history would notice from time to time that he dines with a Mrs. Vanhomrigh—" my neighbour Mrs. Vanhomrigh," at whose lodgings he kept his " best gown and periwig " when he was at Chelsea ; her daughter has a birthday party, but is never mentioned by name. Just perfunctory brief entries, one ending " no adventure at all today." Such a reader would therefore suppose that these were dull people not worth describing who never said anything worth recording. At the same time, while Swift's love and devotion for Stella is apparent and pronounced in so many entries, the reader would notice a very marked falling off in the terms of endearment and the intimate note as time passes. We, however, who can study all that is known of Swift's history are obliged to recognize in these seemingly trivial features the symptoms of what must have been very nearly a tragedy. His visits to Mrs. Vanhomrigh resulted in the remarkable sequel that her daughter Esther conceived an affection for him which we are told actually amounted to passionate adoration, and she even pursued him eventually to Ireland. Such a relationship was impossible without considerable encouragement on Swift's part. We need not, however, embark on the much discussed question of Swift's dubious

10

relations with Stella and Esther, generally referred to as Vanessa, the name given her by Swift himself in his poem *Cadenus and Vanessa*. The subsequent history—the dramatic close of Vanessa's life and Swift's marriage to Stella, which is not authenticated beyond all doubt, are matters about which much has been written, but a recital of them would carry us too far beyond our purpose. We cannot meticulously dissect the Journal in order to ascertain the exact moment of the cooling off. All we are concerned with here is that in this apparently indiscreetly open Journal he was undoubtedly practising concealment and this makes the terms of endearment and his expressions of longing for Stella's company ring false. In fact, with all his fun, we cannot really like him. His journal betrays him and is interesting for that very reason. Superficially a great deal of entertainment can be derived from his daily notes with their strange medley of grave and gay, true and false, malice and kindness.

A couple of complete entries may be given to illustrate the mixture :

I went to court to seek a dinner but the Queen was not at church, she has got a touch of the gout ; so the court was thin and I went to the coffeehouse ; and Sir Thomas Frankland and his eldest son and I went and dined with his son William. I talked a great deal to Sir Thomas about Manley and find he is his good friend and so has Ned Southwell been and I hope he will be sage though all the Irish folk here are his mortal enemies. There was a devilish bite today. They had it, I know not how, that I was to preach this morning at St. James's Church, and abundance went, among the rest Lord Radnor who never is abroad till three in the afternoon. I walked all the way home from Hatton garden at six, by moonlight, a delicate night. Raymond called at nine but I was denied and now I am in bed between eleven and twelve, just going to sleep and dream of my own dear roguish impudent pretty M.D.

I got out early today and escaped all my duns. I went to see Lord Bolingbroke about some business and truly he was gone out too. I dined in the city upon broiled leg of goose and a bit of bacon, with my printer. Did I tell you that I forbear printing what I have in hand till the court decided something about me ? I will contract no more enemies, at least I will not embitter worse those I have already, till I have got under shelter ; and the ministers know my resolution, so that you may be disappointed in seeing this thing as soon as you expected.   I hear lord-treasurer is out of order.   My cold is very bad.   Every body has one.   Night, dear rogues.

The Journal was never intended for publication.   It was written to Stella under a solemn prohibition to show it to anyone whatsoever.   Its preservation is probably due to the fact that in writing his history of the last years of Queen Anne, Swift himself resumed possession of it in order to refresh his memory as to facts.

LADY ARABELLA DENNY

THE manuscript of a diary entitled " Account of my journey from Dublin to London on my road to the German Spa " in 1751 was discovered among the papers of General W. T. Layard. There was no apparent proof of authorship in it. But by internal evidence of relations mentioned, incidents recorded and handwriting it was found to be the work of Lady Arabella Denny. Lady Arabella (or Arbella as she always signed herself), born in 1708, was the daughter of Thomas Fitzmaurice, twenty-first Lord and first Earl of Kerry and Anne his wife, daughter of Sir William Petty. That she was a woman of remarkable character is shown by the fact that her nephew Lord Shelbourne, the Prime Minister, says in his Autobiography : " I am determined if I live a very few years to collect everything I can about her, for her life deserves much better to be examined and recorded than that of Madame de Maintenon, or Madame Roland or even Catherine II of Russia." This determination, however, was never carried out. Scattered fragments with regard to her life have been collected together in a memoir by Miss Amy Percival which, however, has never been printed. At the age of nineteen Lady Arabella married Colonel Arthur Denny of Tralee Castle. According to Lord Shelbourne, who writes with some animus against the Denny family, she suffered a good deal from his cruelty. He died in 1731 and she survived him sixty-one years, dying in 1792 at the age of eighty-four. She was buried in Tralee church, and we learn from the Kerry Magazine (1856) that " the most remarkable circumstance attending the funeral was the wailing of the twelve mourners. These were twelve widows who each received two suits of black yearly and donations at festivals from her ladyship since the death of Col. Arthur

her husband." We must refrain from collecting anecdotes
and records of Lady Arabella's activities and great charitable
work, as we are only concerned here with her brief diary of
travel, which is certainly more picturesque and spontaneous
than the travel journals of a later date.

Her travelling companions were her sister, Lord Chief
Baron Bowes, and later from London Robert Downes, Bishop
of Ferns, and Mrs. and Miss Downes. She begins by noting
the stages of the journey, the number of hours taken and
her expenses. Passing through Oxford she writes :

All Souls college has the fine towers I think so light, so strong and
so ornamental, Rattcliff's Library is a round building highly finished
and very beautiful. The chappel at Queen's College I like best, as
being most solemn.

The Magdeling Building is most beautifully situated, one end to
the park, the other to fields with fine trees and a pleasant water runs
by the building.

We gather from the accounts that they had a certain
retinue of servants with them. The Chief Baron had two,
his sister three, and Lady Arabella two. She gives 10^s 6^d to
" Mr Kennedy Lord Chief Baron Bowes servant who had
the trouble of making all the Disbursements on the Road."
Greenwich she describes, and at Canterbury " we lay at the
Fountaine Inn where the People are civil and the Eating
good " ; Dover " where we drank tea and looked at the
curiositys of the place," and Ostend which " is in my opinion
by no means worthy of a stranger's notice."

The approach to Ghent gives an idea of her appreciation
of beauty :

The entrance into Gent is extremely pretty, a vast number of
wind-mills are at the subbarbs ; the canal from Bruges to Gent was
repairing, but near the Town of Gent it was full of water and made
the coming into the town quite pleasing to the eye. The houses
being painted on the outside with various colours, as the owners fancy ;
some purple and white, some green and white, and so on as fancy
directs : these colors with the mixture of trees and the prospect of
the water gives an agreeable and lively view to the approaching
stranger.

In Brussels she describes many sights and presents a letter
to the head of the English nunnery :

but I had not time to stay in Brussels long enough to receive any other advantage from it than her agreeable conversation for half an hour, she was Handsom, Chearful and told us she was contented.

Before leaving Brussels she makes this general reflection :

By what I have seen in this country Wealth may be ranged among the Regulars confin'd to Churches Convents and Monestrys while Poverty seems at full Liberty you see it on its footsteps in every street and Trade can only be said to breath here (*marginal note* Wealth in this town is a vestal and Poverty a strolling strumpet), By the general appearance of the common people I must take for granted that beauty in this country is a tender plant and requires Housing, the very reverse of England where it seems to thrive most in the open air.

On her way from Brussels to Spa the party dine at " a Little Ordinary Inn full of Bugs." Soon after their arrival they dine with the Prince Bishop of Liège :

We stood till dinner was on the table which consisted of 19 covers and 2 removes at the first course and 19 more at the second and dissert, we stood while the cloath was taken off and the table cover'd with a crimson velvet laced at the edge with gold. . . .
The Prince had at his plate a gold salt cellar cover'd and the knives, forks and spoons with which he eat were of gold, the rest of the table was served with silver plate.

The Prince asks the English ladies to a ball on Sunday :

but on my hearing this I beg'd a Lady who could speak French well to tell the Prince that the English Ladys never danced on a Sonday, on which he asked " What then do they do ? " She answered that they pass'd that day more retired, that after service they either read or made friendly visits and for amusement that day they were used to walk or take the air : he said it was quite right and ordered the ball to be on Monday so that on a Sonday there was not one ball during the season.

She describes the Prince at a ball :

His dress was a long habit of any common color, laced or embroyderd when he was not in full dress, with a small scarlet silk cap at the back of his head ; the heels of his shoes, red, as were all the ribbons to which his various orders hung and his Caul string, and in full dress his coat was scarlet silk, so were his stockins but his hat was black.

At another dinner party " a piece of rost beef " was " the

only thing I cou'd give a name to at the Table." Her description is most elaborate, giving accurate details with regard to the costume of the servants, one of whom :

went round the table with a branch of a Tree in his hand which he held over our heads to beat off the flies which were quite numerous.

Dinner with the Prince of Orange at Aix-la-Chapelle is described down to the smallest particular. She gives full accounts of the picturesque costumes worn by each set of servants who brought in the courses. Of the Prince himself she says :

the Prince who speaks all languages took care that even they who understood but one shou'd not be unentertained. . . . I never saw anyone who was so happy in their address and finding subjects to converse on, with absolute strangers.

Of the nunnery in Aix-la-Chapelle she writes, " I never saw anything more perfectly neat and commodious." No stage of her journey is missed, and she always makes a note of the scenery and the " agreeable prospects " as she passes from one spot to another. Towards the end of the tour, when they are at St. Omer, they hear of the death of the Prince of Orange. " This news dampt our spirits and put everyone on assigning some cause for his death." This is the only note approaching gloom in the whole diary. Indeed, whether she is describing a cathedral or a dinner party, a picture or a " prospect," she manages to instil into her daily entries a sense of great enjoyment, and in the last sentence of the diary she says : " I thank God for having made this journey without one displeasing accident to me or to my company."

We should like to have heard more of the Baron and the Bishop, her travelling companions. The Bishop remains at Spa and does not return home with her. There is a reference to him in her accounts which is much to his credit :

In which expence the seeing places on the road from London to Spa is not included ; the Bishop insisting on my not bearing any part of that disbursement, as he resolved to gratify his own curiosity and would have me believe my being of the party did not enlarge that article of expence.

The extracts have been taken from a typed copy of the original manuscript which has been kindly lent by the Rev. H. L. L. Denny.

exist in which we find that " the flippant and uninteresting

THEOBALD WOLFE TONE

THE concluding years of the eighteenth century are
packed with many exciting events in Ireland and
one might expect to find many diary records of the
period from observers. Curiously enough it is one of the
chief actors who has left part of an autobiography and a
very full diary which he wrote, no doubt, so that posterity
might understand his motives and intentions. Theobald
Wolfe Tone had an astonishing career. Mr. Barry O'Brien
calls him " The Irish Separatist *par excellence*," and the Duke
of Wellington said he " was a most extraordinary man, and
his history is the most curious history of those times. With
a hundred guineas in his pocket, unknown and unrecom-
mended, he went to Paris in order to overturn the British
Government in Ireland." That briefly is what he did, and
the Bantry Bay expedition was the result. He made other
attempts and was finally caught on board a French ship in
1796 and sent to prison, where he committed suicide at the
age of thirty-five. It is certainly curious that a born rebel,
a man of such active and adventurous disposition, should
have found, not so much time and opportunity, although
that must have been difficult enough, but inclination to
write down in great detail day by day his thoughts and
doings. Tone, however, is a conspicuous instance of a self-
regardant egoist who finds the unfolding of the story of his
life intensely interesting. Up to 1789 we have his autobiography, after that full extracts from his diary, the entries
in which were no doubt fuller and longer than they appear
to be in the printed volumes. One of the editors of an
abbreviated edition notes that the diary extracts printed
are taken from " a voluminous mass of flippant and uninteresting matter." This is a good instance of the common

failure of Editors. Fortunately fuller editions of his diary
exist in which we find that " the flippant and uninteresting
material " is in reality the human element which gives the
colour and character, and brings us into contact with the
personality of the writer. Without this the narrative would
be difficult to read.

Tone, who was born in Dublin in 1763, showed his adventurous disposition at an early age. He ran away with his
wife, who was sixteen years old, went off to London, where
he studied Law ; returned to Dublin, where he made the
acquaintance of Thomas Russell, the founder of the United
Irish Society, the object of which was to unite Protestants
and Catholics of Ireland against England. He undertook
with the approval of Emmet and Russell his extraordinary
mission to France in order " to apply in the name of my
country for the assistance of France to enable us to assert
our independence." His diary tells the whole story. Tone
wrote fairly regularly and often very fully, not only on his
projects and his policy, but on the passing events of the
day. This rather slap-dash rebel was very conscientious
about keeping a diary. In January, 1793, he writes :

I find it very hard to keep these journals regularly. I have an
arrear on my hands since the week I left London. I wish I could
bring myself to set apart some certain time for journalizing : but
as that would be something approaching to system I despair of
it.

He kept it up from 1789 to 1798. In Ireland he refers to
all his friends by nicknames, of which a key is given in Mr.
O'Brien's edition. In his description of conferences and dis-
cussions of schemes, he writes with such vivacity and ease
and with constant personal remarks that there is a complete
absence of dryness or effort. The following entry, which he
begins after a break of two months, shows that Wolfe Tone
thoroughly understood the value of regular journalizing :

The only good in my journals is that they are written at the
moment and represent things exactly as they strike me whereas
when I write after an interval of some time—But I am going into
an essay on journal writing instead of my business.

He wrote for a reader, and that reader was his wife, from whom he was so constantly separated. When they are together he stops writing :

Here is an end of my journals now for some time at least. Since I came to France which is now above fourteen months I have continued them pretty regularly for the amusement of my dearest love. As we are now together once more they become unnecessary : we must wait for another separation.

In a letter to his wife he refers to his journal as " a thousand times wittier than Swift's as in justice it ought, for it is written for the amusement of one a thousand times more amiable than Stella."

There can be no question of Wolfe Tone's affection for his wife, judging by the constant references to her in the diary. Later, " We are now nearly twelve years married, and I love her ten thousand times more than the first hour of our union."

There is indeed something epistolary in his style, although not in the form, but nevertheless he had developed the diary habit before he was separated from his wife. He never hesitates to write down his passing thought, however preposterous, and changes it if need be in the next entry. Here is the end of an entry with one of his references to his great friend Thomas Russell, whom he always refers to as P.P. :

One and all of us damn the Government. Home. P.P. sober Find a large packet by the mail which we rip open in haste and find 2000 prospectuses of the United Irishmen instead of the pamphlet. Sat down in a pet and wrote a tart letter to Chambers : got up in a rage, cursed, stormed. P.P. very wise, quotes " Seneca " "Boethius de Consolatione " and many other good books ; enforces the folly of anger in many shapes : I more and more enraged. Left the Inn and went to sleep at Dr. Mc Donnells. P.P. not quite honest ; owes me now several shillings and makes no movement towards payment : gave him a hint on his observing how cheap Belfast was, and that he had not changed a guinea for some days, by assuring him that I had and found it very expensive : hope this may do. Bed.

And in the next entry :

Went to the inn : **P.P.** paid the bill by which my anxiety as to
my shillings is completely removed : believe I owe *him* now two or
three but shall not inquire.

Throughout he was never flush of money. In the midst
of his schemes in France, he writes :

Yesterday I dined with Carnot and today I should be puzzled to
raise a guinea. I am almost on my last louis.

And again later on :

So here I am with exactly two louis in my exchequer, negotiating
with the French Government and planning revolutions. I must
say it is truly original. *Crescit amor nummi quantum ipsa pecunia crescit.* That is not true as to me for my passion increases as my funds
diminish. I reckon I am the poorest Ambassador today in Paris,
but that gives me no great concern. Huzza ! *Vive la Republique* !

It is impossible to follow his intrigues and activities and
it will be best to give some illustrations of his interviews,
his depressions, his gaiety and his almost impertinent candour. The entries are generally very long, only occasionally
a brief one occurs, like " Blank ! Dull as a post all day."
They often start with a reference to health. " Rise with a
headache," " Bed at $\frac{1}{2}$ past 1 damned bad hours," " Rise
sick as a dog " and not infrequently we get something of
this sort : " walk home elevated with liquor. God bless everybody."

His exuberance and depression remind one very much of
Haydon. They make the disentanglement of the actual
course of the proceedings extremely difficult to follow. Here
is an instance of a triumph in Ireland before he left :

Before the debate goes on five minutes satisfied that we **have** it
hollow ; the Lisburn men and our good advisers in the field all
mistaken. More and more satisfied that this *moderation* is nonsense
and stuff. *Carry the question* with about five dissenting voices, among
whom are Joy and Waddel Cunningham. All hollow. Could have
carried anything. The business now fairly settled in Belfast and
the neighbourhood. Huzza ! Huzza ! Dinner at the Donegal
Arms.

Everybody as happy as a King, but Waddel, who looks like the
Devil himself ! Huzza ! God bless everybody Stanislas Augustus

George Washington : *Beau-jour*. Who would have thought it this morning ? Huzza ! Generally drunk—Broke my glass thumping the table. Home God knows how or when. Huzza ! God bless everybody again, generally—Bed with three times three. Sleep at last.

This may seem ridiculous, but it is real diary writing, catching the intoxicated elation of the moment and more than that it is obviously Wolfe Tone. In fact, there are few entries which deal with the complicated rigmarole of his schemes which are not brightened with a description of a dinner, an opera, or the book he happens to be reading :

No business. In the evening the opera as usual *Oedipe à Colone*. More and more delighted with that piece and especially with Adrien in Oedipe. *Psyche* the ballet with Duchenien a charming little woman in *Psyche*. I do love the spectacles of Paris dearly and how much more should I enjoy them if I had the society of my dearest love !

He is fond of branching off into the construction of castles in the air for the future :

I should like very well to be the first Irish Ambassador ; and if I succeed in my present business I think I will have some claim to the office. " *Oh Paris is a fine town and a very charming city.*" If Ireland were independent I could spend three years here with my family, especially my dearest love, very happily. I daresay P.P. would have no objection to a few months in the year at *l'hotel d'Irlande*. He is a dog. Indeed we could discuss several bottles of diplomatic Burgundy.

He gives very detailed accounts of his interviews and in spite of constant delays and rebuffs never loses his fantastic optimism about his projects. After his first interview with Carnot, which he describes at immense length, he writes :

Here is a full and true account of my first audience of the Executive Directory of France, in the person of citizen Carnot, the organiser of victory. I think I came off very clear. What am I to think of all this ? As yet I have met no difficulty nor check, nothing to discourage me, but I wish with such extravagant passion for the emancipation of my country, and I do so abhor and detest the very name of England, that I doubt my own judgment lest I see things in too favourable a light. I hope I am doing my duty. It is a bold measure ; after all if it should succeed and my visions be realised

—Huzza ! *Vive La Republique !* I am a pretty fellow to negotiate with the Directory of France, pull down a monarchy and establish a republic ; to break a connection of 600 years standing and contract a fresh alliance with another country.

Here is a comparatively short complete entry when he is under the reaction of depression :

A sad rainy day and I am not well and the blue devils torment me. Hell ! hell ! Allah ! Allah ! Allah ! Tomorrow I will go and see Clarke about my commission. Will it not be extraordinary to see me in the service of the Republic ? That will console me for the exile I lie under from my native country. It is raining now like ten thousand devils.

Just when one cannot help believing that the man was in reality a charlatan there comes a businesslike description of all the projected operations ; one finds Carnot, Hoche and others taking him absolutely seriously till at last one begins to realize that his weaving of the plot was highly successful. He, practically single-handed, set the machine in motion, and the failure was due to the faultiness of the military machine, not to any deficiency in Wolfe Tone's persuasive powers. His elation seems to be fully justified. His ejaculations and quotations, his exclamations and rhapsodies, interspersed with jokes and rhymes, sometimes annoy him when he reads them over next day :

It is vain to deny it my journal of yesterday is as dull as a post. I think I have not seen anything more stupid and there is a sort of pert affectation of being witty for which I deserve to be kicked. " Gentle dulness ever loved a joke."

The alteration of mood goes on throughout. One day it is " hell ! hell ! hell ! " the next he is " as gay as a lark." Now he says " I am tired of my life," " *je m'ennuye de ma personne,*" but later again : " I think I am growing sprightly once more,"

He is very angry with Hoche for putting the expedition into danger by staying away with a lady. " I never did a foolish thing myself in my life for the sake of a woman," he adds. One evening on board ship, when the expedition is under way, he philosophizes about women :

Having nothing better to employ me I amuse myself scribbling these foolish memorandums. In the first place I must remark the infinite power of female society over our minds, which I see every moment exemplified in the effect which the presence of Madame Ragoneau has on our manners ; not that she has any claim to respect other than as she is a woman for she is not very handsome, she has no talents, and (between friends) she was originally a *fille de joie* at Paris. Yet we are all attentive and studious to please her ; and I am glad, in short she is aboard as I am satisfied she humanises us not a little.

Despondency gains ground over gaiety as events culminate towards hopeless failure. Within sight of Bantry Bay he writes :

There cannot be imagined a situation more provokingly tantalizing than mine at this moment within view almost within reach of my native land and uncertain whether I shall ever set my foot on it.

One would almost expect in the circumstances that Wolfe Tone in face of failure would curse and be unable to write. But, on the contrary, he gives a very full account of events, day by day, and ends up the entry when retreat becomes inevitable as follows :

I confess myself I now look on the expedition as impracticable. . . . It is hard after having forced my way this far to be obliged to turn back ; but it is my fate and I must submit. Notwithstanding all our blunders it is the dreadful stormy weather and the Easterly winds which have been blowing furiously and without intermission since we made Bantry Bay that have ruined us. Well England has not had such an escape since the Spanish Armada and that expedition like ours was defeated by the weather ; the elements fight against us and courage is here of no avail. Well let me think no more about it ; it is lost and let it go ! . . . If God Almighty sends me my dearest love and darling babies in safety I will buy or rent a little spot and have done with the world for ever. I shall neither be great, nor famous, nor powerful but I may be happy.

But, as we know, he was incapable of retiring from active life. In Paris again he is far from happy :

I lead the life of a dog here in Paris, where I am as much alone as in the deserts of Arabia. This night in downright wretchedness I am come to a tavern, where I write this memorandum in a little box by myself. It is miserable. I wonder, shall I ever be so happy as to see my dearest love and our little ones once more ? My mind is overgrown with docks and thistles for want of cultivation and I cannot help it, for I have not a soul to speak to whom I care a farthing about.

The instances of travel notes in the diary are excellent. Tone had the very rare faculty of picking out the salient feature without over-enlarging, of interspersing a description with irrelevant and often amusing thoughts and never giving us the dreary guide-book page which is the general rule. Wolfe Tone meets Buonaparte. This was in 1797, when Buonaparte's reputation was already made.

Buonaparte has " the face of a profound thinker," it is " the countenance of a mathematician rather than a general," he " listened but said very little," " his manner is cold." Buonaparte, who well knew how to measure success and prepare for it, was probably not much impressed by the exuberant young Irishman. Nevertheless, he saw his value. Tone discusses the proposed landing in Ireland and speaks very modestly of himself :

I then observed that I did not pretend to be of the smallest use to him whilst we were in France but that I hoped to be serviciable to him on the other side of the water ; that I did not give myself to him at all for a military man having neither the knowledge nor the experience that would justify me in charging myself with any function. " *Mais vous êtes brave* " said he interrupting me. I replied that when the occasion presented itself that would appear. " *Eh bien* " said he " *cela suffit.*" We then took leave.

Buonaparte is more real and alive in Tone's few sentences than in many of the long-winded pages others have written about him. When Tone reads of Lord Edward Fitzgerald's arrest, he writes in great indignation :

I would rather be Fitzgerald as he is now wounded in his dungeon than Pitt at the head of the British Empire. . . . I cannot express the rage I feel at my own helplessness at this moment ; but what can I do ? Let me if possible think no more it sets me half mad.

The entry on his thirty-fifth birthday, which is almost the last he wrote, begins :

THEOBALD WOLFE TONE

THEOBALD WOLFE TONE 161

More than half the career of my life is finished and how little have I been able to do. Well, it has not been at least for want of inclination, and I may add, of efforts. I had hopes two years ago that at the period I write this, my debt to my country would have been discharged and the fate of Ireland settled for good or evil. Today it is more uncertain than ever.

His end was tragic. Undismayed by failure he accompanied a small expedition which was defeated off Lough Swilly. He was caught, tried by court martial, condemned to death and being refused a soldier's execution, committed suicide.

Without the diary we should have known only of his wild quixotic spirit, but nothing of his evident personal charm.

11

JOHN FITZGERALD

ONLY one year of the diary of John Fitzgerald, a Cork schoolmaster, has survived. He was editor of the *Cork Remembrancer* at the end of the eighteenth century and was a diligent student of current events. The diary is written daily for the complete year 1793, except for the month of October, and although the entries are quite brief, they tell us a good deal about John Fitzgerald as well as what was going on in Cork. In addition to his tutorial work (he notes the occasion on which he begins with any pupil), he made a little money by writing petitions and letters for other people. Public events, the movement of troops, the arrival of ships are duly noted, but he does not neglect the smaller happenings : " Stewart burned my coat at Sandifords which terribly vexed me " : " a new ribbon for my hair," " Patty Chamberlain's gown was stolen," " My fine large brown teapot was broken by Mrs Devitt this night." In April he attends an execution :

Jeremiah Geany, Dan Shea and M Rourke were executed on a wooden gallows near Blackpool bridge for the murder and robbery of Edward Russell 12 May last. Sheriff Clarke only attended the execution. Sheriff Foster was not present. They all walked to the gallows, Rourke first, Shea second and Geany was hanged last. They arrived at the gallows at 6-30. It was a charming evening, dry and the sun shining, though there were several showers in the morning. Johnny and I went to Shinnicks and saw the execution.

The weather charms him far more than the execution shocks him. He was indeed a very keen weather man. In not one single entry is the state of the weather omitted even when he has nothing else to say. The meteorological note generally comes at the opening of the day's entry : "a beautiful soft dry day " or " very dark guttry day hazy weather."

162

Before we have concluded the first half-dozen entries
Fitzgerald's excessively convivial disposition becomes apparent.   The facts recorded are not accompanied by any lamentations, they speak for themselves :

A smart cold day without rain but freezed very smart after nightfall.   Four companies of the 58th marched out of town this morning.
The remainder of the 69th marched here from Kinsale.   Beastly.
Johnnie and I drank 3 pots of Irish porter in my parlour which I
paid for.   This was the first liquor I drank since St Stephens day.

A dismal gloomy dark day with some slight rain after nightfall.
Betty Mackey, Johnnie and I drank six pots of Cork porter between
us.   I fell out with her about her desiring me never to mention anything about Maurice begging my pardon and told her never to come
inside my house again.   She was very hearty.

A cold day with rain and sleet.   Drank too freely last night, when
I went home could not get in.

A gloomy cold day.   Johnnie and I drank two pots of cork porter
and two large jugs of punch royal between us and both went to bed
very mellow.

A beautiful fine sunshiny day, freezing hard.   Mulligan beat me
at cards in his own house.   1s 8d :   I beat him only 5d.   He afterwards treated me to two pots of beer and two glasses and I treated
him to two glasses more at Bat Murphy's.

We hear something of his food too :

Norrywood bestowed on me a nice bit of pickled pork, a pretty
bit of corned beef, three pig's tails and a fine rasher of bacon for my
Easter Sunday dinner.

Coals fell to 7 Irish shillings a barrel this day.   Mutton was 5d per
lb.   Johnny and I ate bacon, eggs and mutton chops for dinner.

He appears on occasions to have made his guests pay for
their food :

Dan Horrigan and his wife dined with Johnnie and I.   They paid
for the mutton chops and peas.   I drank milk after dinner.

Fitzgerald on several days declares that he sees the comet.
This fact seems to have been investigated not only by Astronomers but by Astronomers Royal.   They declare that no
comet was visible in the sky at the time Fitzgerald notes it
and learned scientists and archæologists appear to be mysti-

fied when he writes : " I saw the comet again very clearly."
The matter for surprise, however, would seem to be not that
John Fitzgerald saw a comet, but that after Cork porter
and punch royal he did not see several comets.

The month of October is missing, but in the early entries
of November we find the schoolmaster suffering from some
fearful complaint which is not specified. From his own
account he does not seem to have been either a heroic sufferer
or an easy patient to manage :

Dr Bagnell paid me the fifth visit.

A cold raw morning and a little frost. I was roaring like a bull
all day until 6 p.m. when Dr B. gave me some drops which gave
me instant ease. Betty Mackay staid up all night with me I was
so bad.

We are glad to find Betty bore him no ill will for turning
her out of the house earlier in the year. She probably knew
how to make allowances for Cork porter.

A very heavy fall of rain most of the day and night. I continued
roaring without intermission from 11 a.m. till 3-30 p.m. but being
able to screech no longer was obliged to stop with hoarseness, sore
throat and violent headache.

A heavy fall of rain all the forenoon and none in the evening. I
cut my left thumb this morning slicing liquorice stick. I was screech-
ing and roaring for a long time before and after going to bed.

He gradually recovers. Betty Mackay dines with him,
and he says " got an entire quart of threepenny beer to her
own share." We feel she deserved it after nursing such a
patient. Next day, however, he is taking his share again :

Betty Mackay and Reddy dined with me and drank share of jug
of punch and two quarts of threepenny beer.

The illness passes ; it must certainly have been painful.
If asked to speculate as to its cause we would do so in two
words : " Cork porter." We find Dr. Bagnell taking the matter
in hand towards the end of November. Fitzgerald notes
this in one of his wonderfully comprehensive but compact
entries :

A dismall day almost resembling night. Dr Bagnell gave me a strict charge never to be intoxicated ; not to drink spirituous liquors but very moderately of any kind of liquor. William White tobacco twister abused Johnny about his dog who was going to bite him. Philip Clements killed his wife this day and afterwards cut his own throat.

But the Doctor's advice was disregarded and a short time later he is treated to porter in varying quantities almost daily, and Johnnie and he are at it again :

Xmas Day. A great fog all day, the weather was mild and fair without rain. Johnny and I dined at home and took three pint jugs of punch royal between us. A party of the Tipperary militia went to St Nicholas Church played on their instruments and sang all the Psalms. Alderman Lawton paid me a visit at my own house but sent me neither wine, stout or porter for a Christmas gift. The remainder of the Tipperary militia marched with fife and drum to the North Chapel.

It is a great pity there is not more of Fitzgerald's Diary. It gives both information and entertainment. It is published in the Journal of the Cork Historical and Archæological Society, Vols. 24–26.

DANIEL O'CONNELL

IN the case of Daniel O'Connell, "the Liberator," we have a tantalizing instance of a man who led a stirring and interesting life, and who showed by the early effort he made at diary writing that he had the qualities of an excellent diarist. And yet because he could not decide how to use his diary, never really treated it as a confidant nor as a regular register of his doings, nor as an outlet for his reflections, he did not form the diary habit and consequently stopped.

He began writing when he was studying Law at Lincoln's Inn in 1795 at the age of twenty-one, and continued more irregularly in Dublin till 1802. An elaborate title page shows he intended to make a serious attempt, but he never for long kept up the particular method he from time to time resolved to follow. He makes a resolution "to write something every day," but he only keeps it for a time, and then comes a long break, after which he renews his resolution, but adds :

I know not how long this resolution will last. But this I know : that to persevere in it would be of the utmost utility to me. Did I regularly record the reading of the day shame would prevent me from being negligent. The perusal of my journal would be the best reward of diligence the surest punishment of idleness.

One of the reasons he gives against daily writing, however, is a good one :

After returning from town I put it off for a while then deferred it till after supper. I found it oppress me as a disagreeable task. It in fact occasioned the same sensation which I used to feel when formerly I intended on a particular day to go to confession. Now I mean that this Journal should give me only pleasure and profit.

Therefore I resolved not to write anything that night as I felt writing a burthen.

When he writes "I am now thinking on paper" we wish very much that he would go on in that vein. As to the books he reads, he begins at first by noting down in each of the entries the actual number of pages he reads, much in the same way as Fynes-Clinton.[1] Later he comments on what he reads. On the whole we get a pretty full list of his reading during the three or four years : law, history, science, poetry and very little fiction. Paine's *Age of Reason* interested him, and Godwin's *Political Justice* seems to have made a lasting impression.

He suffers from a fault which diarists are very fond of noting, namely, failure to get up early in the morning. Time after time he registers resolutions to improve. He tries to use his diary also for making character-sketches, but there are only one or two. It is when he is not trying to do anything in particular, when he is just recording something which strikes him or scribbling down the thoughts of the moment that he is at his best. Many of these show already the spirit and ardour of the man as he came to be known in after years. In 1796 he writes in one of the "numbers," as he calls his diary entries :

The man whose mind is not forcibly excited by some object is not capable of receiving any strong impression. He is incapable of love or friendship. Give me the man whose generous mind is inflamed now with an ardent enthusiasm is now chilled with causeless apprehensions. I mean not the apprehension for self which degrades man but the apprehension that arises from excess of desire and anxiety for success. The man who conceives strongly is the man of genius. He is the friend and the patriot.

It would seem sometimes almost as if he had glimpses into his own future when he writes :

I wish I knew how to make a proper estimate of my own talents. But that is impossible. Sometimes—and this indeed happens most frequently—I am led away by vanity and ambition to imagine I shall cut a great figure on the theatre of the world. Sometimes I fear that I shall never be able to rise to mediocrity. But this I

[1] See *English Diaries*, p. 357.

always think that nothing could shake the steadiness with which I would pursue the good of my country. Distant prospects rise unbidden to my sight. They are not unwelcome to my heart.

In February, 1797, he visits the Irish House of Commons. After commenting on one of the speakers, he writes:

I too will be a member. Young as I am, unacquainted with the ways of the world, I should not even now appear contemptible. I will steadfastly and persevering attach myself to the real interests of Ireland. I shall endeavour equally to avoid the profligacy of corruption and the violence of unreasonable *patriotism*. Of real patriotism moderation is the chief mark.

This, although prophetic, is a curious entry because he was disqualified by being a Roman Catholic from entering Parliament at that time. There is no trace of morbidity or unnecessary self-depreciation in entries such as this:

During this year there has been no action of mine which ought to bring regret to my conscience or shame to my cheek.

Yet he wants to correct his faults:

I wish it was in my power to get entirely rid of all propensity to falsehood. I wish I could content myself with simply stating the fact on all occasions. Wilful error is degrading to the mind of the utterer. It lessens him amongst the hearers. I told a lie this night point-blank.

And in another place he writes humbly:

I wish I had that smoothness which society bestows on its frequenters.

The only love-affair which occurs in the diary concerns a lady referred to as Eliza, whom he apostrophizes on one occasion in truly Byronic style. Although he marries only a few weeks after the conclusion of the journal, there is no mention whatever of Mary O'Connell, his cousin, who became his wife. In the same way the Act of Union, of which of course he strongly disapproved, is never referred to. Indeed, there is very little mention of public events. The diary is intimate and personal. The pity is that it becomes so scrappy and irregular. When he begins an entry " I do not mean to write much as my fire is out " we get the close personal touch which is so valuable.

O' Connell's early enthusiasms never take the form of rhodomontade or merely wordy exuberance. They seem to be the early kindling of the inspiration which urged him forward in the work of his life, and in the notable part he played in his country's history. Again and again he refers to his love of liberty :

I love, from my heart I love, Liberty. I do not express myself properly. Liberty is in my bosom less a principle than a passion. . . . The liberty which I look for is that which would increase the happiness of mankind. In the service of that liberty I have devoted my life and whatever portion of talents I may have or acquire.

I love liberty—and this is a moment fit for indulging reflection on the subject—I love liberty as conducive to increase the portion of human happiness. A great deal of the misery of man can clearly be derived from the form of government under which he lives. Oppression harasses his faculties. Privilege confined by *accident* insults his understanding. His industry is consumed to support the follies and vices of men who help him not. When it is exclaimed that "the splendour of government must be maintained," it should mildly and firmly be replied, "No, but the happiness of the people should be established."

The absence of method, the inconsequence and the freshness in O'Connell's writing make a diary so small in dimensions of considerable account in its nature. It was published and edited with full and careful notes by Arthur Houston, LL.D., in 1906.[1]

[1] Quotations from *Daniel O'Connell: Early Life and Journal* are given by kind consent of Sir Isaac Pitman and Sons, Ltd.

JOHN WILSON CROKER

A LTHOUGH in very close touch with the leading political actors of his day and an intimate friend of Canning, Peel and Wellington, John Wilson Croker never himself took any prominent part in politics. He was secretary to the Admiralty for twenty-one years, but he steadfastly refused high office. The bitter controversies which surrounded his name in the literary world served to bring him before the public rather than the help and advice he gave to statesmen and princes.

The estimate made of him by some of his contemporaries may have been unfair. Not only is there Macaulay's attack on him, but Rigsby, the very disagreeable character in Disraeli's *Coningsby*, was intended as a sketch of him.

John Wilson Croker was the son of an official in Ireland and was born in Galway in 1780. He first got into Parliament as member for Down Patrick in 1807.

Croker was more of a recorder than a diarist. He wrote long memoranda of interviews and conversations, diary letters to his friends, and collections of anecdotes and notes on particular events. The scraps of actual diary which remain are meagre. It is mostly objective narrative in the Greville style—curiously formal, almost punctilious in the long descriptions of ceremonials and written obviously for others to read. Nevertheless, the personal element cannot be completely excluded by any constant writer, and there is probably more of this than we can find in the three volumes of the Croker Papers. It would be interesting, for instance, to know what his personal feelings were with regard to his bitter controversy with Macaulay. But if he ever made any diary entries on this subject they are not printed. Mr. Jennings' three volumes are indeed more in the nature of a

vindication of Croker than a Life of Croker. The extracts
he gives, therefore, may have been selected to suit that purpose. Croker we are told did not really keep a consecutive
diary, nevertheless in the periods in which he wrote the
entries are almost daily, and although his intention was to
make an objective chronicle the personal note inevitably
creeps in.

The death of his son was indeed a blow from which he
never recovered. It would have been impossible for him to
put pen to paper with a reader or no reader in view without
referring to it. So he records it and refers to it the following year in the recital of a conversation in which he notes
that he said that :

> I now had every day less and less reason to dabble in such troubled
> waters, for that all my ambition which was never very great, was
> now buried with my poor child and that I did not want and would
> not accept changed office or of rank as any favour. I continue in
> office not because it gratifies me, but because I am advised, and
> indeed feel that having spent all my life from twenty seven to forty
> in office, I should be *désœuvré* out of it, and that, under my present
> feelings I could not answer for my own strength of mind.
> I observe that my nerves, as they are called, grow every day
> weaker and more irritable, above all when I think of my poor boy.

Eight years after the boy's death the entry creeps in in
the middle of his recital of political affairs :

> Our melancholy anniversary I stayed at home. Mrs Croker paid
> her sad visit to Wimbledon.

Several passages indeed reflect Croker's lack of ambition,
his indifference to applause and public success. He did not
want to be made a Privy Councillor, but he gives in and
writes :

> What an empty name is that of Privy Councillor, but as long as
> public opinion designates it as an honourable step, public men must
> consider it so too. I am an instance of this ; I had formerly declined
> it and at last accepted it fully aware of its inanity, only because
> people told me that not to be a Privy Councillor would look like
> degradation.

For just a moment the recorder is self-regardant. Less so
when he records his refusal of office. Thus we get in the

shape of narrative conversation to a certain extent self-revealing but not as his own thoughts and feelings would be. In fact, Croker treated his journal as one of the means (he had many others) of recording history not as a confidant. In his first refusal of office in 1832, he writes that he told the Duke of Wellington :

I had neither birth nor station nor fortune ; nothing but my personal character to hold by and I would leave them to judge what would be thought of me if after the part I had taken, I should be found supporting schedule A of the Reform Bill and accepting a high office and salary as a price of that support.

Of his second talk he writes :

He again pressed me, and much more strenuously than before to take office, and a little surprised me by saying " that in such a crisis as this, if a man put himself on the *shelf*, it might not be so easy to take him off the shelf when he perhaps might desire it." I told him at once rather sharply that " such an observation could not apply to me ; that I had recorded with him as well as with other friends eighteen months ago, my fixed resolution never to take office again ; and that besides all other reasons I really felt that my health could not stand the worry of business ; and that it was with nervous reluctance and the most painful sensations that I went to the House at all ; that nothing but an imperious sense of duty drove me there and that I was quite sure that if I were to undertake the double duties of Minister and debater I should knock up in a couple of months." . . .

Many entries are purely political speculation and party prognostications. There is a curious amount of detailed account of ceremonials. One or two of his descriptions may be given as they have a good deal of merit. He is more gossipy than Greville but less gossipy than Creevy. Queen Caroline, with all the fuss that surrounded her, figures largely but not favourably :

The Queen was at Astley's last night and (was) received as one would suppose *such* a person would be by *such* company as is ordinarily found at *such* a place.

There are immense descriptions of talks and evenings with George IV, far too long to quote. But he gives us the stuffy atmosphere of the Pavilion in 1822 with the King arguing,

singing, playing cards and never going out except to step
across and see Lady Conyngham.   Here he is arguing :

> The King would not agree in this and went off into a dissertation
> on taste and genius. Very clever but rambling. He made some
> really just and critical distinctions but then he, in some passages,
> involved himself to a degree to be hardly intelligible.

Here is a reference to William IV :

> Parliament is up. The King closed the session in person. He
> was received by the people with indifference. The mob observed
> that he *spat* out of the window of the carriage as he went along
> and said " George IV would not have done that."   Kings are but
> mortals and must spit, but I agree with the mob, they had better
> not do so out of the window of the state coach.

Although the majority of the entries are purely political,
social functions and dinner parties come in for some description, with lists of names, and there are several conversations
with the Duke of Wellington.   At a Drawing Room in 1822
he notes " the absence of hoops brings the ladies into such
close contact that some of them quarrelled and were near
pulling one another's feathers."

Croker's letters to Lord Hertford were often in diary form,
but Mr. Jennings' collection is made up of letters and memoranda far more than of diary extracts, and in the latter there
is nothing of his Parliamentary encounters or literary controversies.

TOM MOORE

OBJECTIVE diarists who describe the passing events of their day and the persons with whom they associate are more common than introspective diarists. The value of their record depends to some extent on the importance of the society in which they lived. There is the purely social diary of which Henry Greville's [1] is a poor example, and Henry Edward Fox [2] a good example ; there is the semi-social, semi-political, such as Thomas Raikes' [3] diary, the interest of which soon fades, and the literary social, of which Crabb Robinson's [4] voluminous record is a notable example. However objective the diary may be, the personality of the writer, as well as his style and method, matters very considerably. This discloses itself inevitably because it is impossible for anyone to give a daily account of what is taking place around him without an occasional expression of opinion or reference to domestic and personal affairs.

There is always something rather irritating in gossip and anecdotes about great people. This, as already noted, comes from the fact that some diarists hope to get reflected glory from their admissions of having been on intimate terms with the great. Even when any such motive is absent, it is difficult for a diarist to do this sort of thing well. Haydon [5] succeeded completely, but he was very far from being an objective diarist.

Tom Moore's diary is certainly one of the best examples of this class of diary. He wrote punctually from 1818 to

[1] *English Diaries*, p. 374.   [2] *More English Diaries*, p. 190.
[3] *English Diaries*, p. 369.   [4] *Ibid.*, p. 344.
[5] *English Diaries*, p. 254.

1847. He wrote for eventual publication, as is shown by
his instructions to Lord John Russell, his literary executor.
He wrote well and easily and introduces anecdote and story
perhaps better than any other diarist, because he had a very
discriminating sense of humour.   He realized the possibilities
of diary writing and when referring to Evelyn's, says, " How
I wish every man kept such a diary."   Nevertheless, his
diary would not have reached the high level it does were it
not for the charm of his personality, which is illustrated far
more by the occasional little intimate, and perhaps insignificant details of his domestic life than by his social experiences.
For instance, the following entry which no one culling extracts
from Moore's diary would probably notice, gives by its atmosphere the impression of a man from whom one is very ready
to hear more :

One day so like another that there is little by which to distinguish
their features ; and these are the happiest ; true cottage days,
tranquil and industrious ; with no other alloy than the weak state
of my sweet Bessy's health which I trust Heaven, after she has had
her little one, will improve.   Pursued my task all day in the garden,
the evening most delicious ; seemed to be the last soft farewell of
summer.   The Hugheses came to tea and supper ; played and sung
and read to them Morton's comedy of the " School of Reform."   I
should like much to act Tyke.

There is much that is long-winded in his politics and the
negotiations over the Byron memoirs and their destruction
are described at very great length.   But in the majority of
entries there is a lightness of touch, a gaiety and twinkle,
which make them very good reading.   He is never profound,
he never dissects people, curiously enough he never even
describes their appearance, but he records their remarks and
so in a kind of roundabout way shows us himself through
them.

Tom Moore was born in 1779 in Dublin.   When he began
writing his diary in 1818 he was already a famous poet, *Lalla
Rookh* having been published the year before.   He had also
written a number of political squibs and satires and he was
" taken up " by Society, where his social gifts were highly
appreciated.   He was a frequent visitor at Holland House,

and his cottage in Wiltshire was close to Bowood, Lord Lansdowne's home. Although time may have lowered his literary reputation as compared with that of his famous contemporaries such as Byron, Scott, Wordsworth, Coleridge, Lamb, he was in his day perhaps more personally popular than any of them. To meet Moore and hear Moore sing one of his Irish melodies was an invitation no one could resist.

His singing was a great feature and the following entry shows how much it was appreciated :

I sang in the evening. Stewart I was happy to see much delighted. When I met him some years ago at Lord Moira's I watched him while I sang, and saw him, when I had finished, give a sort of decisive blow to the sofa, which he was reclining against. This gesticulation puzzled me and I could not tell whether it was approbation or condemnation ; but I am satisfied now. I never saw any *man* that seemed to feel my singing more deeply ; the tears frequently stood in his eyes. Miss Edgworth, too, was much affected. This is a delightful triumph to touch these higher spirits.

Sometimes the audience was less satisfactory :

Music in the evening ; all but Mackintosh and the elder Macdonald attentive. They talked the whole time ; I did not mind Macdonald ; but I was sorry for Mackintosh. I said, when I got up from singing, " I see those two gentlemen like to talk to accompaniment " which brought the rest of the company upon them, and they were put to the blush.

A full entry in 1828 will show not only Moore's style of diary writing, with its jokes and anecdotes, but will give a good idea of the sort of active social life he led :

May 23. Rogers having told me he was to meet Scott this morning at breakfast with Chantrey, went there early. Found Scott sitting to Chantrey, with Rogers, Coke of Norfolk, and Allan Cunningham assisting. Talked of Sir Alexander M.—(I think) and his son, on whom the following conundrum was made ; " Why is Sir A. like a lapland winter ? " " Because he is a long night (Knight) and his sun (son) never shines." When Sir W. went away Chantrey begged of R. and me to stay and keep Coke in talk during his sitting to him. Got him upon old times, told a strange story (which I find Rogers more inclined to swallow than I am) of a dinner given by Lord Petre to Fox and Burke after their great quarrel, and of a contrivance prepared by Lord Petre to introduce the subject of their difference, and afford an opportunity of making it up. This was no less than a piece of confectionery in the middle of the table representing the Bastille ! " Come, Burke " said Lord Petre, at the dessert, " attack that Bastille." Burke declined. " Well, Fox " continued his Lordship, " Do you do it." " That I will, by G—— " said Fox, and instantly dashed at it. Credat Judaeus. I doubt much whether they ever met again after that quarrel. Came away with Rogers. A letter from Bowring, informing me that he was preparing copies for me of Lord Byron's correspondence with him ; and, strange to say, opening up at once, without any reserve, the subject of my attack upon him in " The Ghost of Miltiades " ; " you have written bitter things of me " he says. He then expresses a strong desire for a few moments' conversation with me, adding that he thinks he could, in a few words, remove the impression I had of his conduct. Went to Col. Bailey's having promised his daughter on Wednesday evening (in order to get off singing then) to come and sing for her this morning. Found Mrs Wilson, &c. &c. Was in good voice, and with The Song of the Olden Time drew tears from the young beauties around me. Dined at Lord Lansdowne's and finished with the second act of Sontag's Donna Anna, in the Countess St Antonio's box. Not a bad day altogether. Walter Scott, Rogers, and Chantrey, at breakfast ; music and Miss Bailey at luncheon time ; dinner at Lansdowne House, with the Venus of Canova before my eyes, and Sontag in the evening. Taking it with all its et ceteras of genius, beauty, feeling and magnificence, no other country but England could furnish out such a day.

He was impatient if his company was not up to the mark :

Dined with ——, very dull ; but he gave us claret ; et c'est toujours quelque chose ; dulness and port together are the devil.

When there was fun he no doubt was the centre of it. He confesses on one occasion that he talked " I sometimes feared rather too much ; but they seemed to like it and to be amused." His optimism was catching. He does not groan about his sins on his birthday, on the contrary :

May 28. My birthday. What, again ! well, the more the merrier ; at least I hope so ; and, as yet (with all my difficulties) have no reason to complain. An excellent, warm-hearted, lively wife, and dear, promising children. What more need I ask for ? A little addition of health to the wife, and wealth to the husband, would make all perfect. Prepared for my trip to town to-morrow.

The jokes he repeats are very good and very aptly intro-
12

duced. A joke like a jewel wants its own setting ; to extract it is to spoil it. But one or two may be risked :

April 13. (IN PARIS) Dined with Lord Trimlestown ; company, Lord Granard, Lattin, Harry Bushe &c. Lattin and I told Irish stories by the dozen. Some of his very amusing. A posting dialogue ; " Why, this chaise is very damp." " And a very good right it has to be so, sir ; wasn't it all night in the canal ? " Found, on my return home at night, Lord Byron's letter about Bowles and Pope, which Fielding had sent me to look over. The whole thing unworthy of him ; a leviathan among small fry.

April 15. (IN PARIS) Dined at Fielding's ; George Dawson and Montgomery. Dawson told a good story about the Irish landlord counting out the change of a guinea. " Twelve, 13, 14," (a shot heard) : " Bob, go and see who's that that's killed ; 15, 16, 17 ; " (enter Bob) " It's Kelly, sir "—" Poor Captain Kelly, a very good customer of mine ; 18, 19, 20, there's your change, sir."

A note at my hotel directed " To the immortal Thomas Moore Esq ; " only think of an immortal esquire ; expected to hear the chambermaids cry out " Some hot water for the immortal gentleman in No. 18."

a man brimful of ill-temper, coming out of a room where he had lost all his money at play, and seeing a person (a perfect stranger to him) tying his shoe at the top of the stairs ; " D—n you (says he) you're always tying your shoe " and kicked him down stairs.

He greatly enjoyed Sydney Smith :

Turned back with Sydney to call at the Duke of Northumberland's ; left our cards. Told me that he had been knocked down by a coach the other day in crossing the street, and was nearly run over ; and that, knowing how much of Lord Grey's patronage had accrued from accidents happening to clergymen, he found himself saying as he came down " There's a vacancy."

And he tells how he and Luttrell were so overcome with laughter at Sydney Smith that all three are " obliged to separate and reel each his own way with the fit."

But he has serious moods and even fits of the " blue devils." Nature seemed to inspire him to rhapsody, as the two following passages show, both taken from the year 1819 :

Felt bursts of devotion while I walked and looked at the glorious world about me ; which did me more good than whole volumes of theology.

The sunset this evening glorious ; the thoughts that came over me while I looked at it of how little I have done in this world and how much my soul feels *capable of* would have made me cry like a child if I had given way to them ; but surely there is some better sphere for those who have but *begun* their race in this.

His references to people are never descriptions but passing impressions or more often quoted sentences. He meets Mrs. Siddons :

sitting between Mrs Siddons and Lady Castlereagh, I heard for the first time the voice of the former, (never having met her before) transferred to the ordinary things of this world,—and the solemn words in her most tragic tone,—" I do love ale dearly."

His intercourse with Sir Walter Scott is commented on elsewhere.[1] Here is a charming picture of Lord Grey :

it is indeed a noble thing to see this high unbending politician in the bosom of his happy family, playing with the young ones like a schoolfellow and listening to the music of the elder girls with all the attention and delight of a lover. He is, I have no doubt, proud and aristocratic and looks as loftily down upon us untitled ones as the rest of his caste ; but speaking of him in his own sphere, he is a truly noble fellow, and joins more the solidity of the shaft with the ornaments of the capital than any of his caste.

There is an interesting entry in 1834 when Moore, in recording a conversation with Fonblanque, gives his views on the future of literature—views which may make us who live in the twentieth century think furiously :

Broached to him my notions (long entertained by me) respecting the ruinous effects to literature likely to arise from the boasted diffusion of education ; the lowering of the standard that must necessarily arise from the extending of the circle of judges ; from letting the mob in to vote, particularly at a period when the market is such an object to authors. Those " who live to please must please to live " and most will write down to the lowered standard. All the great things in literature have been achieved when the readers were few ; " fit audience find and few." In the best days of English genius, what a comparatively small circle sat in judgment ! In the Italian Republics, in old Greece, the dispensers of fame were a select body, and the consequence was a high standard of taste. Touched upon some of these points to Fonblanque, and he seemed not indis-

---

[1] See p. 2.

posed to agree with me : observing that certainly the present appearances in the world of literature looked very like a confirmation of my views.

There are many entries about dinners at Holland House and visits to Bowood, descriptions of foreign travel with Lord John Russell, the whole of the episode with regard to the Byron papers and his anxieties in respect to the embezzlement by his deputy in Bermuda, which forced him to leave the country for a while. Moore, the social success, is very like other social successes, culling praise, flattered by the friendship of the eminent, having his head slightly turned and thoroughly enjoying the company of those among whom he undoubtedly shone. He retains his modesty, however, and refers to himself as " a little lion." But it is his domestic life, his devotion to his mother, his adoration of his wife, and his sacrifices for his children which give his record the charm which places it on a very different level from other social diaries.

Bessy's presence one can feel throughout. As Maurice Hewlett has said, " Through all the sparkle and flash, under all the talk, through all the tinklings of pianos and guitars which declare Tom's whereabouts, if you listen you can hear the quiet burden of her heart-beats."

The following incident occurred a few weeks after his son was born :

Read the Vicar of Wakefield to Bessy in the evening. What a gem it is ! we both enjoyed it so much more than Joseph Andrews. A man had come in the morning, a young Irishman, and said his wife had been delivered of twins on the road, and was lying without any comforts for them at a house in Sandy Lane ; never could he have found Bessy in a tenderer mood for such a story. She had a large jug of caudle made instantly, which she gave him, with two little caps and two shifts out of the stock she keeps for the poor, a pound of sugar, some tea, and two shillings, one of which was my gift, because he was an Irishman.

Nov. 17. Our Irish friend did not bring back the pitcher as he promised. Suspicions began to arise ; walked to Phipps's ; called at the cottage where the fellow said his wife and twins were lying ; found 'twas all a cheat. Sad hardeners of the heart these tricks are. . . . Read the Vicar of Wakefield to Bessy in the evening.

On April 1, 1819, there is a one-line entry, " Made Bessy turn her cap awry in honour of the day."

On the tenth anniversary of their marriage he writes :

March 25. This day ten years we were married, and, though time has made his usual changes in us both, we are still more like lovers than any married couples of the same standing I am acquainted with. Asked to dine at Rancliffe's, but dined at home alone with Bessy. This being Sunday, our dance, in celebration of the day, deferred till to-morrow.

March 26 (IN PARIS) Bessy busy in preparations for the dance this evening. I went and wrote to my dear mother, and told her, in proof of the unabated anxiety and affection I feel towards her, that a day or two ago on my asking Bessy, " whether she would be satisfied if little Tom loved her through life as well as I love my mother " she answered, " Yes, if he loves me but a quarter as much." Went into town too late to return to dinner, and dined at Véry's alone. Found on my return our little rooms laid out with great management, and decorated with quantities of flowers, which Mrs Story had sent. Our company, Mrs S. and her cousins, Mrs Forster, her two daughters, and Miss Bridgeman, the Villamils, Irving,[1] Capt. Johnson, Wilder, &c, and the Douglases. Began with music ; Mrs V. Miss Drew, and Emma Forster sang. Our dance afterwards to the pianoforte very gay, and not the less so for the floor giving way in sundry places : a circle of chalk was drawn round one hole. Dr. Yonge was placed sentry over another, and whenever there was a new crash, the general laugh at the heavy foot that produced it caused more merriment than the solidest floor in Paris could have given birth to. Sandwiches, negus, and champagne crowned the night, and we did not separate till near four in the morning. Irving's humour began to break out as the floor broke in, and he was much more himself than ever I have seen him. Read this morning, before I went out, Thérèse Aubert, and cried over it like a girl.

On the death of their daughter he writes :

On the 12th our darling child was conveyed to Bromham churchyard, poor Bessy having gone the night before to see where she was to be laid. Almost all those offices towards the dead which are usually left to others to perform, the mother on this occasion would perform herself, and the last thing she did before the coffin was

---

[1] Washington Irving (1783–1859), the American essayist and historian, who spent a great part of his life in Europe, and appears frequently in these memoirs.

closed on Wednesday night, was to pull some snowdrops herself and place them within it.   She had already, indeed, laid on her dead darling's bosom a bunch of cowslips, which she had smelled to (and with such eagerness) the day before her death, and it was singular enough, and seemed to give Bessy pleasure, that though lying there three days they were scarcely at all faded.   I had ordered a chaise on the morning of the funeral to take us out of the way of this most dreadful ceremony, (well remembering how it harrowed up all our feelings in following my poor father to the grave), and a most melancholy drive we had of it for two long hours, each bearing up for the sake of the other, but all the worse, in reality, for the effort.

And such is the end of so many years of fondness and hope ; and nothing is now left us but the dream (which may God in his mercy realise) that we shall see our pure child again in a world more worthy of her.

In 1830 :

September 6.   Drove into Kilkenny, with Bryan and Bessy.   In looking along the walk by the river, under the Castle, my sweet Bess and I recollected the time, when we used, in our love-making days, to stroll for hours there together.   We did not love half so really as we do now.

His son Tom was a cause of trouble :

Have just found the note my poor Bess wrote to me, in sending up to town Tom's bill upon me for £112.   " I can hardly bring myself to send you the enclosed.   It has caused me tears and sad thoughts, but to you it will bring these and hard hard work.   Why do people sigh for children ?   They know not what sorrow will come with them.   How can you arrange for the payment ?   and what could have caused him to require such a sum ?   Take care of yourself ; and if you write to him, for God's sake let him know that it is the very last sum you will or can pay for him.   My heart is sick when I think of you, and the fatigue of mind and body you are always kept in.   Let me know how you think you can arrange this."   The difficulties to which this bill of Tom's reduced me were considerable : and I had not been more than a week or two at home, when another bill of his, drawn upon me at three months, for £100, was sent to me for acceptance.   This blow coming so quick after the other, was, indeed, most overwhelming.   It seems on his arrival at Bombay, he found that his regiment had been ordered on active service, and he was accordingly obliged to provide such an outfit as would enable him to join it.   I could not do otherwise, of course, than accept the bill ; but how I am to pay it, when due, Heaven only knows.

None of his children survived him. There is too little of the quiet uneventful days about which he shows he can write so well. With readers in view he seems throughout to be thinking that they will want to hear more about the great world. On two uneventful days he just writes " *Niente, niente,*" which, of course, was not true.

Moore lived to the age of seventy-three, but his last years were harassed by debts and the misconduct of his sons. Before he died the buoyant, friendly, brilliant spirit became a total wreck. Even in the concluding entries of the diary in 1847 there are signs of confused thought.

The diary is given in full in *Memoirs, Journal, and Correspondence of Thomas Moore,* edited by Lord John Russell (1855), and a judicious selection with an excellent introduction by Mr. J. B. Priestly was published in 1925.

JOHN MITCHEL

THE Jail Journal of John Mitchel has a place of its own among diaries owing to the circumstances in which it was written. There are other prison diarists no doubt, both in this country and abroad, but with the exception of the concluding portion of James Hannington's diary [1] no British civil prisoner's notes seem as yet to be available. In most cases indeed the monotony of strict confinement would hardly inspire a victim of the law with a desire to note his daily experiences with regularity or fullness even if he were allowed to. Mitchel's varied and exciting adventures bore no resemblance to the dreary routine of incarceration within the four walls of a prison cell; and his desire, therefore, to keep a record of events was only natural. Moreover, he was a journalist and an agitator. His experiences were good copy and could be converted into good propaganda.

John Mitchel was born at Dungiven, County Derry, in 1815. Ater working as a solicitor, he came to Dublin and became editor and chief writer of the *Nation,* at one of the many periods when the political and social position in Ireland had reached a critical point. His outstanding abilities and strong character brought him to the front, and he became first a supporter and then leader of a movement not only for Repeal but for resistance both passive and active, on the part of the peasantry, against the British Government. Although his agitation failed more, owing rather to the apathy of his fellow-countrymen than to the strength of the forces against him, as he fully recognized, it was Mitchel's policy which was adopted by the Land League thirty years later. The career of this active leader brings us straight into the

[1] *English Diaries,* p. 418.

184

dangerous and tangled labyrinth of Irish politics, from which, however, we can turn away, as we are not dealing either with his career or with his policy, but with his diary. It will be sufficient to say, therefore, that Mitchel's influence was so greatly feared by the Authorities that he was arrested. To charge him with treason did not appear to be sufficient to meet the case. Accordingly he was charged with felony, convicted by a packed jury and condemned to transportation.

He began his journal straight away :

May 27. 1848. On this day, about four o'clock in the afternoon, I, John Mitchel, was kidnapped and carried off from Dublin, in chains, as a convicted " Felon."

He kept up the Journal at first daily, then more irregularly, and at times with long breaks till November, 1853. He also continued in a more fragmentary fashion afterwards. He published the Journal in 1854 in *The Citizen*, a newspaper he edited when he lived in New York after his escape ; and in the same paper he published further extracts at a later date.

The fact that the Journal was written with the intention of publication is modified by Mitchel's ignorance from the outset as to what his fate was going to be and his constant misgivings as to whether he himself would survive. It is never as human or spontaneous as the private diary of a person of no account on whom no public gaze is fixed. Nevertheless, circumstances and adversity threw him very deeply into himself and often as he wrote he faced the profound problems of human existence. When life is uneventful he writes, " Shall I go on scribbling ? " Later he fears his journal may be seized by the authorities, as by that time it had assumed considerable dimensions, so he prepared to throw it into the sea, " using means to load the little book so that it may go to the bottom." As it turns out, he manages to preserve it to the end.

In the earlier part, of course, he bursts out from time to time, more especially when he comes across a newspaper, into political invective against the British Government, who are referred to always as " the Carthagenians." He is bitter and satirical. At times in his frequent use of the vocative he reminds one of Cobbett, although he has not the same humour. He writes a long disquisition on the French revolution of '48, and when in 1853 he gets news of the troubled state of Europe, he waxes eloquent in his hopes that somehow Ireland may benefit by the course of events :

who can tell what the chances and changes of the blessed war may bring us ? I believe in moral and spiritual electricity ; I believe that a spark caught at some happy moment may give life to masses of comatose humanity. . . . Czar, I bless thee. I kiss the hem of thy garment. I drink to thy health and longevity. Give us war in our time, O Lord !

Mitchel was a man of culture and snatched at what books he could reach, and often discourses at some length on authors and their works. A violent diatribe against Macaulay occupies several pages. Having an active and cultivated mind, he resents being cut off from any intellectual stimulus :

I never dream of killing Time for fourteen years—if it came to that Time would kill me—fourteen years would be too many for me. . . . Therefore, I intend, after having been at grass a while to cultivate friendly relations with Time—a thing to be done by *Working* only—to get old Time on my side instead of living *against* him.

He goes on to project the writing of a book. But owing to circumstances this plan never materialized. He writes about his health, his sleepless nights from asthma, and he is very naturally addicted to depressions. The descriptions of his life when lying in a hulk off Bermuda are detailed and graphic. He writes daily and brings the scene which surrounds him with great skill before the reader. Surrounded as he was by convicts, he finds that special treatment is accorded to him which though welcome is embarrassing :

Sunday. Service on deck the prisoners all in clean frocks and trousers arranged on forms over the deck forward ; the guards and mates on the quarter deck amongst whom I had a seat apart. I attended service for a little variety ; also to see what kind of Chaplain we have. After service the Chaplain came to me ; he politely offered to lend me books and even to procure me books from others.

I rather like the man : he did not cant as so many of these persons do but seemed realy desirous of serving me so far as the rules would allow him. He is a Scotchman.

B—— his b—— eyes ! What is he but a convict like the rest of us—a d——, b—— convict ? *Meaning me.* I heard this exclamation today through the wooded walls of my cell, when the gangs were in at dinner hour ; for they sometimes grow loud and energetic in their discourse, and then I cannot but hear some of their words. A b—— convict like the rest ! The man is right ; and I am well pleased to hear the observation and to see the black scowls that some of the prisoners give me when any accident brings them to meet me on the pier. By " Act of Parliament " and by the verdict of a " Jury," I am a felon as they are and know no title I have to walk about " like a gentleman " that is idle while they work hard. Right my felon friend I like to know that such a feeling is astir. . . . I honour their cursing and venerate their black looks, trusting that their wrath will fructify into an intelligent and wholesome hatred of those damnable " institutions " which make so much of gentlemanhood and so little of manhood—to wit, the glorious British Constitution in Church and State.

One day he ruminates on the fourteen years of his sentence and he argues out the question of suicide :

Suicide I have duly considered and perpended and deliberately decided against, for reasons which I will here set down in order so that I may have them to refer to if that method of solution become a question with me hereafter ; for alas I know that in fourteen years will be many a dreary day many a weary night ; and sickness and deadly *taedium* will fall heavily down upon my soul ; and often the far off end of my days of sorrow will be clean out of my sight for the thick clouds that will seem closing around me, veiling all my horizon in the blackness of darkness.

He then proceeds to give six reasons against suicide.

Mitchel, however, never discloses himself in his diary very intimately. With all his apparent volubility he is really reticent. The Journal is public, not private. When, therefore, after three years, the longed-for and prayed-for moment arrives when his wife and children join him in Tasmania, the entry is almost the briefest in the whole journal :

June 20. 1851. Greenpounds. Today I met my wife and family once more. These things cannot be described. Tomorrow morning we set off through the woods for Bothwell.

His flowing pen, the practised pen of a journalist, fairly
runs away with him in many entries. The scenic descriptions are not very good and occasionally there are passages
of truly appalling journalese, like the following :

For nearly six years I have been shivering at the extremities,
whereunto slender capillaries brought but trickling drops of life,
where the systole and diastole could hardly be felt to throb ; and
where the old Earth " o'er the embers covered and cold " borne in
ships from far-off fires, has to warm her frosty finger.

But on this occasion it is only fair to say that he corrects
himself by adding :

The above reflection is partly nonsense, yet not all nonsense. The
pen of scribbling mortals running recklessly in chase of a metaphor,
plunges, but too often unwarily, into the quagmire of balderdash.

In his fatal facility for scribbling, however, he has one
great quality which, considering the events he has to record,
is of special value. His powers of narrative are of a very
high order, and he depicts scenes, incidents and personalities
with striking and photographic clearness. Whether he is in
the hulk off Bermuda, waiting outside Cape Town while the
anti-convict agitation is proceeding on shore, or wandering
in the wilds of Tasmania, his daily descriptions convey to a
reader with great realism the particular atmosphere which
surrounds the diarist.

But undoubtedly the most arresting part of the Journal
is his attempted, and eventually successful, escape from Tasmania, which lasted from January to November, 1853. We
may again note here that the Diary form is specially well
suited for the narrative of this type of adventure. Although
a reader may know beforehand the successful or unsuccessful
issue of the schemes and plans, the Narrator as each day he
relates the projects, the ventures, the thwarted plots, the
hairbreadth escapes, is, as he writes, completely in the dark
as to what the morrow will bring. His ignorance imparts a
reality and a breathless suspense which no writer, calmly
recording the sequence of events in retrospect, can possibly
imitate. Mitchel tells the story each day of consultations
and calculations, of strenuous hardships and repeated failures,

with elaborate detail and direct simplicity of language, although he cannot resist occasionally indulging in this sort of remark :

Already I begin to sniff the air of the upper world and to see daylight through the opening gates of Hades.

" Our plot is blown to the moon " he records one day, and the next another is hatched. Perhaps the most exciting moment is his visit, accompanied by a companion known as "Nicaragua," to the magistrate of the district, previous to his escape. We must give a bit of this in his own words :

Still he made no move and gave no order. So I repeated my explanation : " You observe, sir, that my parole is at an end from this moment ; and I came here to be taken into custody pursuant to that note."

All this while there was a constable in the adjoining room, besides the police clerk, and the guard at the door ; yet still his worship made no move. " Now, good morning, sir " I said, putting on my hat. The hand of Nicaragua was playing with the handle of the revolver in his coat. I had a ponderous riding-whip in my hand, besides pistols in my breast-pocket. The moment I said " Good morning," Mr Davis shouted, " No—no ! stay here ! Rainsford ! Constables ! " The police clerk sat at his desk, looking into vacancy. We walked out together through the hall ; the constable in the district constable's office, who generally acts as his clerk, now ran out, and on being desired to stop us, followed us through the court, and out into the street, but without coming very near. At the little gate leading out of the court into the street, we expected to find the man on guard on the alert between us and our horses. But this poor constable, though he heard the magistrate's orders, and the commotion, did not move. He was holding two horses, one with each hand, and looked on in amazement, while we passed him, and jumped into our saddles.

We concluded that we had done enough, and that there was no reason to wait any longer. Mr. Davis and two constables rushing against one another, with bare heads and loud outcries—grinning residents of Bothwell on the pathway, who knew the meaning of the performance in a moment, and who, being commanded to stop us in the Queen's name, aggravated the grin into a laugh ; some small boys at a corner, staring at our horses as they galloped by, and offering " three to one on the white un "—this is my last impression of Bothwell on the banks of the Tasmanian Clyde.

But this was by no means the end. He has to disguise himself as a priest, to wander in the wilds and to pass the night in an open boat.   These passages are far too long for quotation, but all the adventures faithfully recorded at the moment make a thrilling story.   On arriving at New York on November 29, 1853, he lays down his pen with, " and here ends my Journal."

The subsequent portions of the Journal are summaries of periods and accounts of his activities in America where he took the side of the South against the North and again suffered a term of imprisonment.   In 1874 he returned to Ireland and was elected to the British Parliament by the people of Tipperary.   Although the election was annulled, he was re-elected, but he died a few days later at his old home at Newry.

The Journal, in book form, was published in 1914, with a preface by Mr. Arthur Griffith.

INDEX
OF DIARIES AND CHRONICLES
NOTICED IN THIS VOLUME